Live in the Spirit World

Story of Patricia

Psychography of
VERA LÚCIA MARINZECK DE CARVALHO

English Translation:
Evelín Solís
Lima, Peru, July, 2023

Live in the Spirit World

Original Title in Portuguese:

"Vivendo no Mundo dos Espíritos."
© Vera Lucia Marinzeck de Carvalho, 1993

Revision:
Giancarlo Carrasco Rojas

World Spiritist Institute

Houston, Texas, USA
E–mail: contact@worldspiritistinstitute.org

Live in the Spirit World
Contents

PREFACE 7
1.- NEW FRIENDS 9
2.- THE COLONIES 15
3.- CHARITY AND LIGHT SHELTER 24
4.- OBSERVATION STATION 38
5.– SAMARITANS 49
6.- DISINCARNATION 59
7.- DISENGAGEMENT 67
8.- REINCARNATION 75
9.- CAUSE AND EFFECT 84
10.- ACTION AND REACTION 92
11.- MADNESS 102
12.- OBSESSION 112
13.- REQUESTS 124
14.- THE DOORWAY 136
15.- GETTING TO KNOW THE DOORWAY BETTER 148
16.- DEVICES AND MINDS 158
17.- EARTH'S CREATION 164
18.- CONFERENCE AND THE SPIRITIST BOOK FAIR .. 170
19 - ADDICTIONS 178
20.- ACKNOWLEDGMENTS 191

~ 3 ~

Live in the Spirit World
SYNOPSIS

This is the follow-up of the book *"Violets on the Window"*. In this book we can get to know the author a little more, a simple spirit, but full of love for life. This love translates into the happiness of being a revelation of the God who is the Creator. Patricia, its author, narrates with the simplicity that is proper to her, her walk in the World of the Spirits. She talks in detail about the study she made to find her new home. It was her path which lead her, and will lead us, to know and understand the Doorway, the Colonies, the Aid Stations, the reincarnation, the disincarnation, and the Law of Cause and Effect, and others. (Patricia's Collection Volume 2).

About the Medium

Vera Lúcia Marinzeck de Carvalho (São Sebastião do Paraíso, October 21 -) is a Brazilian spiritist medium.

Since she was a child she became conscious of her mediumship, through clairvoyance. A neighbor lent her the first spiritist work she read, "The Spirits' Book", by Allan Kardec. She began to follow the Spiritist Doctrine in 1975.

She received works dictated by the spirits Patricia, Rosângela, Jussara and Antonio Carlos, with whom she started in psychographic, working for nine years until the release of her first work in 1990.

The book "Violetas na Janela", by the spirit Patricia, published in 1993, has become a best seller in Brazil with more than 2 million copies sold, having been translated into English and Spanish and adapted to theater.

This translation of "Live in the Spirit World" is one more volume in the series "Violets on the Window" dictated by her niece Patricia, all of them translated and available through the *World Spiritist Institute*.

Live in the Spirit World

PREFACE

Since ancient times, the history of humanity has brought us news of basically two characteristic types of men: the heroes or saints, and the wicked, both with their consequent rewards or punishments.

The storytellers do not tell us about the millions of men who come, live, pass through the Earth and leave no traces. Men whose lives have been diluted in the middle of the multitudes. Men who, with their work and dedication, permitted the heroes to accomplish their great works. Men who have come and lived under the pressure of society or practically enslaved by the most astute. During these millions of years, humanity has not yet practiced the good life, except for a few.

In this book, we have in the main character someone who lived properly, when he was in the physical world.

Although he was an ordinary person, his fraternal life was the cause of a calm and smooth passage to the astral world, because it could not be otherwise. Readers will have the opportunity to confirm the enchantments of life, following this character, even though she is neither a heroine or a saint.

Live in the Spirit World

One will see the beauty and harmony of life, when man spontaneously finds himself with cosmic integration. Life gives her child vitality, joy and love uncontaminated by earthly passions.

For the main character, the affection and love of someone who was his father for a not too long period of time.

José Carlos Braghini,

São Sebastião do Paraíso, MG – 1993

1.- NEW FRIENDS

Full of enthusiasm and joy, not for that passing euphoria that occasionally happens to us in the world, but a permanent state that surrounds us beauty in all the things we see and touch, with that state of mind I presented in the department of the school to which I was assigned. I went in alone, crossed the playground and walked towards the area where I would be informed about the course that was about to begin. The little I knew about this course left me eager to do it. I walked into the room where we were to have the first group meeting. As I passed through the classroom door, I saw that many people had already arrived, and everyone greeted me. Greetings accompanied by a sincere smile and loyalty, which I appreciated very much in my relationship with my colleagues when I was incarnated. The room was big and comfortable. The desks or tables were comfortable, and each had a badge with the candidate's name on it. I looked for mine and sat down to wait. Soon all the students arrived. I did not know anyone, but everyone was friendly. I felt like I was among friends, and not superficially, rather among those people in whom we can trust our most intimate affairs. Common in all places where expectation prevails, there were small groups formed in healthy conversation.

- Attention please!

Live in the Spirit World

The three councilors came into the room. We sat down and were silent.

- I am Raimundo.

- I am Isaura.

- I am Frederico.

The three instructors introduced themselves and stood in front of the group. Instructor Raimundo explained that he was going to call everyone together so that we could get to know each other and, if we wanted to, we could say something about ourselves. That this attitude would shorten our mutual knowledge, making us a family. I felt full of life and illusion, I was back to doing what I liked so much: studying and getting to know other activities in this new way of life. In the earthly home, I had heard many explanations from my parents about changing interests and needs outside the physical body, but my expectations were higher now than then.

There were thirty people in the group, seventeen men and thirteen women. The roll call and my turn began.

I am Patricia, I was disembodied at the age of nineteen due to a brain aneurysm, and I've been in Colonia for six months. I love everything here and I'm looking forward to learning.

In the group, she was the most recent discarnate and the youngest in age. There was another student who had been disincarnated for less time and had been in that condition for three years. Most of them had been in the spiritual plane for a long time and had many years of work.

Live in the Spirit World

Mrs. Isaura, a madam with a vast knowledge about the world in which we now live and who has been guided in this course for a long time, gave us, with a kind look and a pleasant aspect, some explanations.

- This course is offered in three ways. Juniors and the older children have it as part of the Education Center study.

The adults can do this in two ways. Those who have no knowledge, do it over a longer period: in three years.

those who have knowledge do it in nine months, as is the case with you here.

Frederico and Mrs. Isaura sat down. Frederico was a friend of mine and would be our instructor. I was glad to see him and have him around. Raimundo answered some questions and, smiling, talked a little about himself:

- I have been on the spiritual plane for sixty years. Fifteen years teaching courses. In each course I learn a little more. Now I am available for questions in this very enjoyable class group.

Marcela was the first one to ask.

- Will we only know the spiritual plane through courses?

- Certainly not. Many people know him through their work. But the courses give us a more extensive and complete knowledge. After a pause, our teacher continued tenderly:

- You will like it. First, you will receive theoretical classes on a given topic and then you will have practical classes in which, through excursions, you will see what you have studied in class.

Live in the Spirit World

In these excursions, you will not only be spectators, rather you will also perform. We will work wherever we are.

Also, we will visit environments designed and supported by ignorant spirits and visit islands of relief maintained by working spirits. We will come back here for discussions and appreciation in which everyone will give opinions and suggestions that will be studied and can be used. Everyone's opinions will be important.

Since nobody asked any more questions, Mrs. Isaura explained:

- In class, you can come dressed as you wish. but on field trips, we will wear a uniform. Clothing is important; for us it's like an introduction. You will find uniforms in your accommodation. Now we will get to know the lodging, your rooms, which is where you will stay while you study here. During the course, between one subject and another, you will have a few free hours. It will be nine months without breaks. In two hours, we will begin the course, and the first subject will be the Colonies. Take these two hours to get to know each other better.

We formed small groups and the three instructors left, they would also stay in rooms like ours and with the students.

- Hello, I am Nair. I don't know anyone here - A pleasant madam–looking sad, speaking to me. - I came from another Colony for this course.

- Nice to meet you, Nair, how about going to see the lodging together?

Live in the Spirit World

I smiled, encouraging her. I didn't know anyone either, but I was going to and I felt I would like everyone. Nair had come from a small colony. She wanted, like everyone else, to learn. We left the room and soon after there were the rooms: there were thirty in a row. There was a nameplate on the door for each participant. I went into mine to leave all my few belongings. I was excited, the room was beautiful. I would stay there for many hours over the next nine months. I love having a place to pray, meditate, be alone to think and so the knowledge gained provides an environment for my spiritual understanding, which is essential for me. The room was ideal, painted light yellow, with lace curtains at the window, which overlooked a flowery garden. It was furnished with a closet, bed, sofa and desk. Beautiful lamps and a wonderful painting of a landscape with mountains and lake adorned it. The bathroom was small, everything was beautiful and comfortable. I put the pictures of my family that I had brought with me on the desk, along with the objects I use for writing and studying. I looked at the pictures for a long time. I love my family and having them on display is very nice. It seemed that they all greeted me with affection and encouragement. My father seemed to say, "I am proud of you, daughter, to know, to learn, is to always have new opportunities."

My family is my delight, together we participate in harmony with the Creator. I kept a few clothes in the closet. The uniform was hanging. It was light blue pants, a blue printed shirt, with my name embroidered on the pocket. The men's shirt was blue, as were the pants. The footwear

Live in the Spirit World

consisted of blue sneakers or shoes. Comfortable and practical, I liked it very much. After looking at everything, I went happily out into the playground. Everyone in class was talking animatedly. We were all together. I entertained myself. I liked them all. At fifteen minutes before the course started, we all went into our rooms to be alone for a while.

It's difficult to describe what I felt, because I always loved to study, I always longed to learn. There I was for my first intensive learning course. I knew a lot from Spirits books what the Spiritual Plane was all about, but now I was discarnate and would see for myself. I prayed and was grateful. I just had to be thankful for the opportunity.

When I heard a soft bell, I went to the classroom. Raimundo was the one who welcomed us:

- My friends, let us say a prayer asking Master Jesus to be our best advisor in this course where we will learn about the Spiritual Plane. That our Great Brother may always be with us and that we may learn, help, throughout his life. Our Father...

With a pleasant smile he gave his first class.

2.- THE COLONIES

The instructor Raimundo began his explanation by informing us of the existence, all over the Earth, of spiritual colonies. There are countless throughout Brazil. The Colonies are cities in the Spiritual Plane that temporarily house the disincarnated spirits who are in the process of reincarnations.

They are lovely! Everywhere there are material cities, there is a spiritual space and there are Aid Stations and Colonies. The small localities where incarnates live, such as villages and cities, also have their spiritual space, except that sometimes there are no Colonies and their residents, when they disincarnate and, if they have conditions, go to the neighboring Colonies.

The Colonies can be small, medium, large and study Colonies.

The study Colonies are just a school or university. There is accommodation for teachers and students, classrooms, libraries and huge video rooms. They are places where scholars dream of meeting and living.

The other Colonies have the same bases, they are enclosed, there are gates, defense systems, big hospitals, schools, gardens, main squares, places for meetings and lectures, and governance. These are not the same and could

Live in the Spirit World

not be the same. All of them are beautiful and offer many attractions.

We watched movies about Colonies, first the many in Brazil, then the main ones abroad. India and Tibet have charming Colonies, with a different architecture, where the color of gold is very light. They are beautiful.

The theoretical class was interesting. There were lot of questions were asked, and the instructors answered with pleasure

- Who founded the Colonies? - Marcela asked.

- Each Colony has its founders. They are groups of building spirits that came to Brazil with immigrants. The same way cities were formed on Earth, so were the Colonies. There are Colonies in the East, thousands of years old. We live in groups, the more advanced helping the more always close to each other. That is why each city on Earth has a corresponding spiritual nucleus.

- Before we colonized Brazil, were there no colonies? - Louis asked.

- Not like these. There were, yes, spiritual centers, in which the guides of Brazil, already planning the colonization, protected and guided its inhabitants, the Indians.

- Can a spirit enter a colony, trying to trick it? - Luíza asked

- We have never heard of such an event. What would he come in to do? He himself would feel bad about not being in their midst. If he wanted to spy, what he would not be able to see he could not copy. He would not be able to, because

Live in the Spirit World

their way of life differs from ours. Almost all the Colonies, the spiritual cities, are certain at a vibratory distance from the earthly orb and, without comparing them with the physical measurements, they are in the fourth vibratory dimension, starting from our beloved Earth.

- If a material city were destroyed, would the Colony also end up in that space? -Ivo asked, curious.

- It would not. If the incarnate's city was not rebuilt, the Colony would move to another location.

- Do the Colonies grow too? - Gloria asked.

- Yes, depending on your needs, they are extended.

- Anticipating a disastrous event in the material city, the Colonies preparing to receive the victims? - James asked.

- Certainly, as well as the Aid Stations in the region, but, in order not to cause panic and concern among its residents, this preparation is done hours in advance.

The practical class began. First, we took a tour of our Colony, which I already knew. But it was, as always, exciting to walk through it. A feast for my eyes and my spirit. Now, with the first group of classmates, the wonderful things I knew seemed to renew in my eyes. Like the mother who never tires of gazing and admiring her loved child. The joyful group learned everything, we saw the parks, the gardens and the buildings. We spoke pleasantly with the head of the Colony, its governor, who encouraged us with kind words. When we visited the hospital, we talked with the patients, trying to convey the joy we felt. We helped with the cleaning and feeding of patients.

Live in the Spirit World

The Colonies maintain a perfect exchange among themselves and with the Aid Stations subordinated to them.

Frederico explained:

- Now, you are going to see the Regeneration School. Not many Colonies have these schools.

They are for dark brothers and sisters to recover. It should be clarified that there is a great difference between dark spirits and spirits in need. Our Spiritist Centers, normally, the needy or ignorant spirits are helped. These dark spirits go very little to Earth, they aren't interested in the incarnated people because they think they're ignorant and useless, there are certainly some exceptions. These brothers almost always dedicate themselves to reign in their domains in the Doorway. There are few centers dedicated to indoctrinating this kind of spirit, as they require a lot of work. They're realized in evil and want to live in evil; they despise any fraternal attitude, they cultivate selfishness.

They dominate and are dominated, there's no freedom. In these domains there are judges and avengers in the name of God. This school was founded to receive these brothers.

The Regeneration School is very beautiful and is located inside the Colony of São Sebastião.[1] It's surrounded, and it's only possible to enter and leave through one door. In it, classrooms and lodging are located, both for teachers and

---

[1] Note from the Spiritual Author: In my first book, *Violets on the Window*, I described the Colony where I am and, in general, all the Colonies. In this book, in order not to be repetitive, I describe them superficially.

Live in the Spirit World

students, a equipped library, a small video room where there is television and movies on various subjects. There's a cafeteria, a lecture room, attendance rooms, an infirmary and the administration. In the back, an orchard and grain fields, a popular place for student therapy. In the center, a beautiful garden with many flowers and benches.

The teachers, in addition to being good, in the fraternal sense, have a deep knowledge to deal with the brothers who are there.

The course is intensive, with classes in Christian morals, literacy and education. The students wear uniforms and only leave the school after finishing the course; they do not go to other parts of the Colony. At the end of the course, they choose an occupation or are reincarnated. It's beautiful work and has given excellent results.

Unfortunately, for these brothers who have spent a long time in error and darkness, an appropriate place is needed for them to receive special guidance. We talked to some students who had been in the school for some time, all were happy; they said that they loved the school and the teachers and that they were enjoying their lesson

It's a great regeneration job!

We went on excursions to other Colonies. We traveled by airbus. We visited a medium-sized Colonia. The Colony of the spiritual space in the city of Ribeirão Preto. It's pretty! Very flowery and its library is huge. It was wonderful to visit this research site which is their library. I was delighted with their old books and videos of the formation of the Earth. It

Live in the Spirit World

has three large hospitals and many parks. The children's area or Children's Home is very large and beautiful.

In theory class, we were asked to visit *Colônia Nosso Lar* ('Colony Our Home').

- My dream - said Luís with enthusiasm - since I was incarnated, is to visit *Colônia Nosso Lar* and, if possible, to see André Luiz.

When the long-awaited day arrived, we went to visit the *Colônia Nosso Lar*, in the spiritual space of the city of Rio de Janeiro.

I think that almost all spiritists dream of knowing this Colony, it was the first one that psychographic described to the incarnates. We were properly received. We spent two days in one of its schools. We got to know all its most important parks and forests. Truly, our *Nosso Lar* is magnificent!

I was thrilled to see so many beauties. On the second day, in the afternoon, we were delighted to meet the writer André Luiz. We met in one of his halls to talk. There are several in this Colony. The hall is round, the scenery is half-moon shaped, the seats are also rounded. The whole room has different shades of yellow. Very beautiful and different. The auditorium was full, several groups of tourists were there for the same purpose. We were told that André Luiz, whenever possible, responds to requests like this, for tours of students who want to meet him. Luís could not stop smiling.

- How delighted I am! My dream has come true! I have been a fan of this writer since he was incarnated!

Live in the Spirit World

André Luiz presented himself with naturalness and simplicity. He is like certain people you look at and find super pleasant. He greeted us smiling.

I thought he was different! - exclaimed Ivo - You're so simple that he does not seem to be so well known by all the colonies in Brazil and by all the spiritists!

Mrs. Isaura looked at Ivo, asking for silence. André Luiz spoke, in a strong, calm voice, that he was only a simple student at a previous stage and that he only became known for having had the opportunity to dictate the books that were psychographic, describing the Spiritual Plane.

The most important thing for him was that all those who were there, wanting to study, should learn how to be useful with wisdom. He then gave a beautiful prayer. The meeting lasted for twenty minutes. Admirer of the duo André Luiz and Chico Xavier, it was a pleasure to hear and see him.

We passed on to one of the Colonies in the city of São Paulo. Altogether there are three large ones. We were with their size - it was properly divided! We also went through Brasilia. A new Colonia, well distributed, modern and wonderful. It's one of the most beautiful Colonies in Brazil. Its squares and gardens are fabulous and there are many flowers of the superior plane that perfume the air, enchanting everyone.

In the program of our Visits there were two Study Colonies. Now it was my turn to be radiant, because these Colonies hold a delightful fascination for me. They are for

Live in the Spirit World

studies only and offer spectacular ways of transmitting knowledge to their students.

- Hello, Patricia - said Nair -, I bet you will go to a Study Colony as soon as possible.

- Yes - I answered smiling and dreaming -, if possible I will study in one!

The Colonies are marvelous indeed. Even trying as we might to describe them, we cannot convey the beauty we see. Each description is also narrated by someone who, through affinity, talks about what he or she likes the most.

Murilo, a fellow nature lover who loves Botany, said that, if he had the opportunity, he would narrate the beauty and variety of plants and flowers. I may find it easier to describe places of study. I love to learn.

We eagerly returned to the classroom, full of spirit and willingness. Opinions were warm.

There were no suggestions, change what? Everything was perfect!

It was suggested that everyone should comment on what they saw and felt on the tour. On the occasion, I spoke with delight of the video rooms, which I have already described in the book Violets on the Window, at the Study Colony. Their themes are complete. Seeing them and making use of these rooms is any learner's dream. The Study Colonies have beautiful and evocative names. I also spoke enthusiastically about the opportunity I had to get to know a perfect society, governed by love and fraternity.

Live in the Spirit World

- Well, everyone liked it, this is good, because in the next topics you won't only see wonders. And the work will be part of the next excursions - said Mrs. Isaura affectionately.

3.- CHARITY AND LIGHT SHELTER

The Aid Stations, said Raimundo, are places where the rescued spirits have a temporary stay, receive support and guidance, and are free to choose the path to follow. If they adapt to a new life and awaken to grow, they will study in the colonies they need. If they are dissatisfied and disgruntled, they return to their place of origin. These Stations are also called homes, mansions, shelters, colonies, etc. Those are smaller relief sites on the crust and on the Doorway. It can be large, medium or small. Although there are some that have all the characteristics of one, these are not cities.

- Do they also have someone who administers them? - Ilda wanted to know.

- Certainly, at the stations, harmony and discipline reign. There's a person in charge and a group of mentors who help in this administration.

- Are the transitional, rotating or revolving houses Aid Stations? - Luis asked.

- Yes, those shelters located within Doorway move, as needed, to other locations within Doorway. These are Aid Stations.

Live in the Spirit World

- What are Aid Stations actually? - Luíza asked.

- They are temporary shelters, where needy brothers and sisters are housed and where their illnesses and needs are treated with all affection. These brothers are taken to the Colonies. However, when they are healthy, many of them remain in the Stations that serve the community that protects them.

We asked a lot of questions, and we watched several movies about Aid Stations. The time has come to visit them.

Frederico introduced us to a Chinese man named In-AI-Chin. This is a friend who will accompany us every time we go on excursions.

We were quiet, but questions boiled in our brains; Zé could not stand it and asked:

- Why is there a reason for us to have such pleasant company? The Chinese smiled softly and Frederico answered:

- There's never been an unpleasant accident on these field trips. You are right, Zé, there is a reason for this companion to be with us. We have Patricia in our midst, who, when she incarnated, was a Spirits, and her father is an indoctrinator, leader of a Spirits Center. As all those who kindle the Light disturb the ignorant brothers and sisters of the darkness, as a precaution, In-AI-Chin will accompany us. Our friend works in the discincarnated of this Spirits Center, he has a lot of experience. He is very fond of Patricia and worked spiritually by her side, when she was incarnated. Always wanting to see her properly, he will accompany her and us on the excursions, which will be the first one for

Live in the Spirit World

Patricia. Patricia's mother fears reprisals for the work her father does; she asked for it and, to reassure her, she was assisted by this friend who will be part of our team.

I thought, "I hope she doesn't turn out like my nursemaid." In-AI-Chin smiled charmingly and....

- I hope I am not being inappropriate. My goal is to help and learn. Even though I've come to be close to Patricia's Blue Flower, I want to be friends with everyone.

I turned red. The group liked his idea. They surrounded him. In-AI-Chin is serene, sweet, of medium height, wears a light robe and a hat. Many spirits like to continue dressing as they did when they were incarnated. I've never seen an enlightened spirit in extravagant clothing. They are simple, they dress as they like. Eastern spirits generally dress in robes, that's how they dress when they're incarnated. It's how they like to be. In-AI-Chin always smiles, showing much tranquility and happiness. She addressed me only as Blue Flower of Patricia. And Zé asked:

- Why do you call her Patricia's Blue Flower?

- Because she has the bluest eyes I've ever seen, also because they are sweet and calm, like two flowers who look at her. Since her name is difficult to pronounce and since she only addressed me this way, we called her Blue Flower, a name that made him happy. He says:

- Nothing more beautiful than to be compared to a flower!

The first Aid Station we visited is at the gentler Doorway. We went by airbus. We saw pieces of the Doorway,

Live in the Spirit World

which I will describe when we go to visit it. What I knew about the stations and what I saw in the lecture made me curious to know what this part of the Spiritual Plane is like.

A large, heavy gate opened, and we entered. Mrs. Isaura exclaimed, moved:

- We are at the Shelter Charity and Light!

The airbus stopped in the courtyard and we got off. The shelter looks like a point of light, of clarity, in the dark fog of the Doorway. It's a place of love! The station has a rounded shape, in the center there is a square with a beautiful fountain. It has many trees and flowers like those that exist on earth. At the entrance, just beyond the door, we see beautiful clusters of colorful roses. All around the stall are large vases with small, fragrant, delicate red flowers - beautiful!

It's surrounded by high, strong walls and has an excellent defense system. Nair, seeing everything, exclaimed:

- This Station must be uncomfortable. You cannot see properly here. Raimundo smiled and explained:

- We that walk for the well we do not attack any brother, nor his cities or shelters. The ignorant dark ones attack us and, if they could, they would destroy this shelter and all the Aid Stations. Yes, we are inconvenienced. Most of the residents of the Doorway do not want help here.

The shelter's director came to greet us with great affection. We were chatting happily when a Station worker approached me.

- Are you Patricia, the daughter of Mr. José Carlos?

Live in the Spirit World

- Yes, that's me.

Without my reaction, he took my hand, kissed it and handed me a bouquet of flowers.

- I owe a lot to your father. I thank him through you. Thanks. I thought of helping you, but since you don't need help, accept this gift.

I was a little embarrassed and for a moment I didn't know what to do. Everyone was watching the scene. I quickly thought of what my father would do in the face of this event. I smiled and hugged him.

- It's good to see friends here! How are you?

- Now I am well, thank God. I work here -, he said proudly, "I owe this to God and your father. I was rescued and guided by him.

- I'm glad to hear it.

The man was moved, wiped his tears and walked away. Mrs. Isaura approached him and said:

- Don't be shy, Patricia. It's touching to see grateful people. Those who do for themselves. His father helped him without expecting a reward. But he, that hard worker, he learned well, and he's grateful. He was happy to see you and be able to thank you. You did right, daughter, we should be grateful and receive gratitude with affection!

A worker showed us to the lodging. We would stay three days and wouldn't leave the room.

They accommodated two in each room. I stayed with Nair. This friend is curious and watchful.

Live in the Spirit World

- This bed is yours, and this one is mine. Will we even sleep?

- As we were told, here we might need to rest, because in this job we donate a lot of energy.

The room was simple, unadorned, with a window overlooking the courtyard and it had a bathroom, because sometimes, when we ate, we needed to use it.

We were called to see the outside of the shelter. Everything is painted white, its windows are shaped like old windows, they're large and working. At the Doorway, outside the shelter, the temperature was cold; whereas, at the Station, it was nice and pleasant. There is a system like a central heater that controls the ambient temperature, so that those in the shelter don't feel cold or hot. We don't feel the temperature change, because we learn to regulate ourselves. For those in the know, the temperature is always mild. Walking through the Station, it seems that we are inside a large construction whose buildings are separated by courtyards. We went to the guard tower. Leonel, a boy who was at the controls, showed us everything. The system is perfect.

Through the devices in the tower they know who is approaching the Station. Everything is televised, the entire defense system is controlled from the tower.

- Does the shelter receive many attacks? - I asked.

- An average of three a month - Leonel answered attentively.

- Have you ever been afraid of one? - asked Zé

Live in the Spirit World

- Six months ago, they gathered in a large group from the Doorway and attacked us with full force. They surrounded us, and we had to put all our lightning launchers into action. The shelter staff concentrated on prayer. I was scared for a moment and thought we would have to ask for help from another Station. But everything went well, they did not even come near the shelter.

- Do you stay here all the time? - Luíza asked.

- We rotate schedules. I love this tower

- Everything here seems complicated - said Luis.

- No, everything is simple, yet perfect.

There is a screen, like a TV, which shows the whole wall.

- Here - Leonel showed -, through this device I can see who is approaching the shelter, three kilometers away.

- What do you do when you are being attacked? - asked Gloria

- First, I alert the shelter, then I turn on the defense devices that shoot electric charges.

- What's this? What's in here? - Luis asked, showing some small objects in front of a TV set connected to the image of a man reading the Gospel.

- This is espionage - Leonel smiling -. Some dark brothers, curious to know what is going on and how it is here, place these listening devices, like buttons, rings, belts, amulets, on the brothers who will receive help. Take a good look.

Live in the Spirit World

We saw it without touching it.

How incredible! - Gloria exclaimed.

We took these devices and placed them in front of this TV. It is tuned to a channel where the Gospels are read daily. The listeners will hear a little of what's in the book and only see what's happening on TV. I knew this channel, it's from a higher sphere where they read and explain the Gospel. It's widely watched throughout the Colony. But the questions continued. Cida asked:

- Is it not possible to keep some of these devices on the rescue?

- No, because they change their clothes and bathe here, but if they stay, they will not see anything that might interest them.

I left the tower feeling very confident. In the courtyard, we divided the group into three parts with ten members plus an instructor and went to the wards. We visited the refugees who were already getting better. I thought to myself, "They are so bad that I cannot even imagine the worst ones."

Men and women looked like ghosts from a horror movie. We pitied them. Thin, bulging eyes and moaning.

Their sorrows were heartbreaking.

I tried to be cheerful as I approached them. I thought that, if I observed them well, I would read their thoughts, as I had read in André Luiz's books, when I was incarnated. I got nothing, so I asked Frederico why - Patricia - he replied - this is for those who know, who worked for years with

Live in the Spirit World

brothers in this state. Soon they will have classes in the course and learn a little about it.

We ate and cleaned the protégés. We talked to them, some responded, explained how they were, some talked about their reincarnating. Usually, they like to talk about themselves, to complain. One sad man said he was cheerful but reckless, made mistakes, suffered a lot when he was disincarnated and was sad. We gave them passes, prayed for everyone we visited. Most of them seemed oblivious; the nervous ones calmed down after the pass.

Some didn't understand anything they saw and asked what was going on, others responded with monosyllables to the questions. By the time we finished, we were tired. We went to our rooms. I showered and went to the dining room, where we ate fruit and drank juices.

It was getting dark. We were invited to go to the music room. The place is very nice, with beautiful paintings, flower pots, and comfortable chairs. Raimundo explained:

- In this room we have television, movies, musical instruments. It's the place where workers and guests gather for edifying conferences.

Maria and Tobias, two workers at the Station, provided us with beautiful melodies, she on the piano and he on the violin.

Marcela, our colleague, sang two songs. We had a pleasant time.

The whole Station is illuminated with artificial light, and even during the day there are lights on inside the

Live in the Spirit World

buildings, except in the courtyards which only have the lights on at dusk. At night, the Station is well lit. We went out into the courtyard. We saw the sky almost like the incarnates, but with more fog, the moonlight is weak. The scent of flowers, especially red ones, invades the courtyards.

We went to rest, I was tired and slept for five hours. At dawn we woke up, ate a meal and visited the resting place of Charity and Light.

- Hi guys! " said Zé, who woke up late. I haven't slept that much in a while.

- When we lose energy and we are not used to it, we need to restore it – Mrs. Isaura explained.

The Station has a beautiful and well-kept library, which contains a vast amount of spirit literature. The good books of the incarnate have their copies there. It is well frequented by workers and the people in recovery. Next to the library is the prayer room. It is a Discrete and very beautiful place, not big, but comfortable. It also has comfortable chairs and flower pots. There, inmates in recovery go to pray. The workers also enjoy attending the room.

It's quiet and has a lot of energetic fluids. There is a lot of peace inside.

The sunrise at the Station is beautiful, the sun appears through the clouds, illuminating the patios and gardens.

We went to the wards. We visited the brothers, who were sleeping in nightmares. Ah, how the harvest is obligatory!

Live in the Spirit World

Seeing them, we were filled with compassion, because we knew that they were all there in that way, because of imprudence, many mistakes. We spent hours in the wards. Seeing so many suffering brothers saddened me. Although knowing that's nothing unfair, we wanted to recover everyone. But this is impossible, because recovery is slow, we helped few. We gave passes, we accommodated, we gave water, we made prayer circles. Only two woke up and were taken to another room. They wake up scared, many fear and cry.

I was tired. Then we went to the room, where I showered, ate, and did breathing and relaxation exercises. We were leaving the next morning. The class would meet in the afternoon to watch a movie and listen to a lecture.

I asked to rest; many in the class did too. Those suffering brothers wouldn't leave my mind. I was reviewing everything like in a movie. The instructors always stayed with us and worked the hardest, always ready to clarify any doubts. Blue Flower, always calm, would help the sick with great affection. After praying, Nair and I went to sleep. Sleeping disincarnated is like falling asleep incarnated. When you're incarnated, the body rests, disincarnated, it's the perispirit that rests, and we re-energize. Right after this course, I never slept again. It's great to have so much time.

Once again, I woke up refreshed. We left without saying goodbye, because we would come back again and again and stay there, while we visited the Earth Stations.

We went by airbus to the crust. Seeing the sun without the fog was much more pleasant, and we breathed a sigh of

Live in the Spirit World

relief. We would visit the existing Aid Stations for the incarnates in that region. In the cities of the Earth there are many small Aid Stations, and in the Spirits Centers. These stations are real points of love and help.

We visited them for hours. We help them by taking care of the sick and the newly disincarnated. Most of the recently disincarnated rescuers remain at the stations for some time, after which they're either taken to be indoctrinated in the meetings in the Spirits Centers or they go to other places and are transported to larger Stations or Colonies.

Those who stay almost always go from being helped to being helpers. There are always many workers and the work are immense. The movement is great; the person in charge of the Station stays to attend to the people and workers who have problems. The stations in the Spirits Centers are always full. Most of them are above the material construction. There is a defense system, door or gate, barred windows, wards, a reception room, a resting place for workers, sometimes music rooms and small libraries.

Nair commented to me:

- Notice, Patricia, that wherever we go there are always good books and many copies of the Gospel and The Gospel according to Spiritism.

- Those who do not want to are not instructed! - I answered her.

- Do you know how many Christians, or those who call themselves Christians, have a religion and don't know the Gospel? - Ivo asked us.

Live in the Spirit World

- There must be many; they do not know and don't follow it, to note by the many rescued - I answered.

- What a pity! – Ivo exclaimed -. The Gospel shouldn't be read but be lived! We were in a stall, all busy, when we heard Cida shouting. I was so frightened that I froze for a few seconds, then I also ran. Cida was in the front room, the dressing room. Frederico arrived so fast that he ran into Blue Flower.

- Calm down, Cida! What happened? - Frederico asked.

- A man came in here, stole a plaster and ran!

- Uff! - Frederico exclaimed with relief.

- I think I screamed (shouted) for nothing - said Cida, embarrassed

- In vain and scandalously, Cida - said Mrs. Isaura affectionately -. There was not needing to shout.

- I apologize - said Cida.

- The brother who took the tape will not pass through the door, only if the doorman leaves. And they often do. He came here wanting objects to make a bandage, sometimes on himself or on his companions. Around the Earth, around the Stations, there are always many brothers wandering around, they are taking advantage of the incarnated. Many take advantages of alcoholics and fight. Sometimes they come here to make bandages, but they know they will hear some truths that bother them, so they prefer to rob us, explained a Station attendant, who finished in a good mood. I hope the scare is over.

Live in the Spirit World

- Do you get a lot of attacks? - Ivo asked.

- Not many. There are more attacks from brothers who want to have fun, but as our electric beams are strong and give them the impression of death, they hardly attack us.

- How did this man get here? - Luíza asked curiously. He is known to the doorman and to me. He asked the doorman to be served, and he also let him in and out without any problems. Most homeless people often ask us for things, like medicine and food, and it's rare that they steal from us. Today, I decided to do so.

José de Arimatea, our distracted Joe, exclaimed loudly:

- I know why we wear uniforms! It is so we do not get confused with the other birthers!

The scare passed, and we went back to chores. It was already dark when we returned to Charity and Light for a well-deserved rest. We made these visits for two days and rested at the refuge. The visits were very useful. I really enjoyed these Aid Stations among the incarnates. They are helpful, where charity is truly applied.

Live in the Spirit World

4.- OBSERVATION STATION

In the morning, we set off again, but this time on foot. Walking through the Doorway is strange. While the Colony is a feast in my eyes, the Doorway, with its anguished and depressing atmosphere, is a terrible and horrifying sight for me. I knew that many spirits wandered there, and I pitied them, just as I also knew that many liked it, which I found distasteful, but we all have free will and everyone likes a place. We walked for hours at a time, all together: Mrs. Isaura at the front, Raimundo in the middle and Frederico at the end; Blue Flower by my side. We did not talk, we walked in silence. We had not recommendations to speak, not to be noticed. We walked cautiously on firm ground, because there was a lot of mud. We wore brown capes, with hoods that reached to our knees, leaving only the face out, and we put on special boots. Luíza commented as we dressed:

- Why do we dress like this to walk through the Doorway? It looks so weird.

- We are just protecting ourselves - Mrs. Isaura replied

- If we are attacked, the cloaks will protect us. The boots are for walking safety.

As I walked through the Doorway, I understood why we dressed like this.

Live in the Spirit World

The Doorway is dirty, and some parts are slippery. The boots gave us firmness and the capes comfort.

Overwhelmed by what I saw, I often found myself wide-eyed. I thought: "If I were here alone, I would be scared to death, if that were possible." At one point, a large bird flew close to us. I was startled and stifled by a scream that got stuck in my throat. But it wasn't just me Luíza and Nair snuggled up to Blue Flower, who was calm and looked at us smiling. The rest of the way I stayed close to him. We made the journey in perfect silence and without any problems.

There was little light, it seemed like dusk among the incarnates. Not much mist or fog. From a distance, the Station just looks like a wall, you cannot see anything of it from the outside. As we got closer, we saw the gray wall and the gate, which looked like a heavy wooden gate, carved in relief, beautiful and simple.

Mrs. Isaura rang the bell and the heavy gate opened. We entered the courtyard: it was square with few flowers in a few flowerbeds, surrounded by small trees without much beauty, like many of those like many that the incarnate possess. We were welcomed by the administrator, director or person in charge:

- Good afternoon! I am Guillermo. Welcome to the Observation Station. Please come with me, I will show you to your quarters, because I suppose you would like to rest.

The Colonies and the Aid Stations continue at the same time as the Earth. If it were two o'clock in the afternoon in the city of the Incarnate Ones, it's two o'clock there too.

Live in the Spirit World

The Observation Station is located at the Doorway, in an area of great suffering. It is a transient or revolving house, that is, it changes location. Joaquim, one of our colleagues, had worked there for years and was away to take the course. After completing it, he will return to his activities. He was greeted with joy, embraced by the Station workers.

We realized that everyone there loved each other, forming a big family.

Artificial lights illuminate the Station day and night. From the courtyard, we went to the guest area. Luíza and I stayed together in the room, which was simple, unadorned, but comfortable. After cleaning up, we went to the coffee shop, where we had dinner, which consisted of fruit and broth. We met shortly afterwards in the conference room to talk.

We were given explanations about the Observation Station.

- This shelter was created while a settlement was formed for the incarnates. When the atmosphere starts to get too heavy, the firestorm arrives, and we change locations, Guillermo explained.

- I wanted to see one! - James exclaimed.

- We are not expecting one for now - continued the Station manager -. The fire falls like lightning burning everything, purifying the heavy fluids. Everyone flees, and those to be rescued are given shelter here.

- Are they moving far away? - I asked

Live in the Spirit World

- No, we have always stayed in the region. There are houses like these in other Colonies, moving to places twenty to fifty kilometers away. We usually move seven to ten kilometers.

- Have you been working here for a long time? Nair asked. Thirty years ago

- Wow! – Marcela exclaimed. You must have gained a lot of experience. How did you get to the Station?

- When I was incarnated, I was a good person who fulfilled my duties. I loved and loved the Gospels and I did my best to follow the example of Jesus. I became disembodied and, when I was rescued, I was taken to a Colony. I found everything I saw there charming, but I loved this Station as soon as I visited it on an excursion, like the one you are doing now.

I understood that there are few who, like me, are helped when they disincarnate, and I felt pity when I saw so many unwise brethren suffering. I wanted to work in the Observation Stations. My application was accepted and during the years I served here, I did a little bit of everything. I was able to help friends, relatives and, little by little, all the rescued became my brothers. Here I learned to love everyone, as Jesus taught us. I have a special love for this help corner. I've been managing the Observation Station for thirteen years.

Guillermo, when talking about the Observation Station, was bright-eyed with enthusiasm. I looked at him in awe, certainly his job wasn't easy. He was there only for the

Live in the Spirit World

love of his fellow men and he showed it in his manners, his calm and kind look. Everyone admired him.

The conversation continued, and we exchanged ideas about the Doorway, about the part we saw. We talked until eight o'clock and retired to our rooms. In the Colony, I hardly ate or slept. Walking along the Doorway and helping at the Stations made us tired, we expended energy. So, we needed food at least once a day and rest. This rest was reading something uplifting, meditating and even sleeping for a few hours.

The other day, at five o'clock in the morning, we participated in the morning prayer. Guillermo invited Mrs. Isaura to say the prayer. Our counselor prayed with a fervor that moved us. Transparent petals of fluids fell on the Station and on us, strengthening us, saturating us with much energy. Soon after, we went to visit the Observation Station. It's a medium-sized station. It has a conference room, also used for music, a directors' room, a cafeteria, a courtyard, consultation rooms, workers' quarters and infirmaries. Our three instructors, since our arrival, have been in the consultation rooms, attending to confused refugees seeking guidance. Blue Flower was helping in the rooms all the time.

We were divided into groups of seven and went with the employees to help in the wards. They are long, with beds on both sides, simple bathrooms, all very clean and bright. The protégés have needs: they eat there and use the bathroom. They're hungry and thirsty, they simply don't feel cold or hot because the Station has a system like the air conditioning of the incarcerated. This system is central,

Live in the Spirit World

leaving the Station, and even its courtyards, at a pleasant temperature.

First, we went to the wards where the patients were in better condition.

We talked to them and helped them feed and clean themselves.

- You are beautiful! - said a very thin woman with sad eyes, addressing me.

- Thank you. How are you?

- I cannot complain now. I have suffered a lot, but it was deserved. When I was incarnated I did a lot of mistakes.

I just smiled. I knew that curiosity leads to nothing. We had recommendations to encourage the sick, to talk about the Gospel and Jesus. But also, to listen to their outbursts.

- You are so good! Did you suffer when you disincarnated? - she asked me.

- No, I felt I was going to sleep, and I woke up well and among friends.

- Among friends. To have friends you must make them, right? I didn't, and the ones I thought I had been worse than I. I bet you did not suffer, because you were good!

- Maybe I should have been better. But I did not make mistakes, I disembodied in peace and harmony accompanied me.

- Do you not want to listen to me for a little? Sometimes I feel like talking. The workers here are great, but they are so busy. You know, I was not good at anything. I was

Live in the Spirit World

a bad daughter, I ran away from home at the age of thirteen to practice mercurial. I had many miscarriages. I had three kids, I gave up two, the other one I would have given up too. He was a cunning child, a thief. One day, when he robbed a client of mine, he killed him. I wasn't a good mother. I drank too much, I grew old fast and death sought me out for suffering. I spent seventeen years at the Doorway. When I was helped, it was a disaster, I was very tired. I have been here for a long time.

- And it will get better soon - I said, encouraging her -. Take from the mistakes of the past lessons for the future. Try to recover and go from being helped to be a helper.

The lady smiled sadly. I gave her a pass, said a prayer out loud, she thanked me:

- Thank you!

A gentleman kept saying:

- Coffee, I must pick the coffee!

After passing, he said bigger phrases, and it was clear that he stole a lot of coffee from his bosses. He harvested coffee from the plantation during the day and stole it at night. The repentance made him see the deed without contemplation. He went to sleep calmly after the prayer circle.

And so, many had real stories to tell, discovered mistakes upon mistakes. Many had been selfish.

They have loved the material more than the spiritual truths. Pride and selfishness lead many to the wide door of

Live in the Spirit World

doom, into suffering after disembodiment. When we left the rooms, Zé commented:

- I was in the mood to ask Frederico about why there are so many wards and, in them, so many needy.

I discovered this by listening to these unfortunates. You know, I was impressing to learn of a man who raped and killed his own eight-year-old daughter.

One of the Station workers, overhearing, argued:

- These are the reckless people Jesus was talking about. They did not do good, they lived for matter, planted evil and reaped suffering. And they did so much evil to others and to themselves, that they could only stay as they are.

So, dear students, these shelters are balms for them.

In the second ward, the patients were in the worst state. Some of them talked non-stop. When they were with food, passes and prayers, they would improve, sometimes they would calm down, sometimes they would speak more coherent sentences.

One gentleman caught my attention, and remorse punished him: he expelled his parents, who were already old, from his house, and they died in an asylum, without seeing him again. Another lady talked endlessly that he had been killed. Having passed, she remembered the lover she had coldly murdered. Another gentleman remembered with anguish his lover's refused daughter.

"That's good! - I thought - haven't had so many mistakes to haunt me. That's how happy I'm! There is nothing better than to plant the good."

Live in the Spirit World

We visited two halls on the first day. The station workers do not do what we did.

There is no time, because there are too few workers for too much work. We finished in the afternoon, going to our room, then to the coffee shop, and from there we went to the music hall.

We went out into the courtyard in the evening. The walls surrounding the vigil are strong and high, and in the playground, there is a tower with the defense system. An elevator is used to get there. We climbed up in small groups. The tower is thirty meters long.

They also have perfect defense systems and never an attack worries them. Margarida, the woman in charge at that time on duty showed us some devices that measure vibrations outside the Station in a radius of three kilometers. They report who is approaching and how many there are. You can't see the sky or the stars; sometimes the moon, when it's full. I looked from the top of the tower, around the Station, I saw nothing, just the station below and its lights; outside, fog and darkness.

When she waited my turn to climb the tower, she looked distractedly at a small, beautiful green stone fountain, with delicate flower outlines, surrounded by plants. Blue Flower approached:

- What are you thinking, Blue Flower de Patricia?

- I look forward to seeing the tower. It was good to see you. I want to thank you.

Live in the Spirit World

-Do you remember the gentleman who thanked you at Charity and Light shelter? I feel the same way, only happier, because I can accompany you and do something for you. What I do to you, I would like to be doing to your father too. A lot I owe to him, to the Spirits group and to you. Just to be able to give back is a grace. I have been your friend since you were incarnate. Do not thank me, I do it from my heart and with happiness.

- How nice to be your friend, Blue Flower!

- When we have good friends, we have treasures. Having you and your father as friends makes me feel rich.

He smiled tenderly. "Yes - I thought -, he is right. Having good spirits as friends is having spiritual treasures. Also, I felt that I had great goods."

Frederico said his evening prayer and we went to rest. I was thinking about the sick, what I saw and what I heard from them.

Oh, how wickedness does evil to the wicked! It's hard to get the harvest from the bad sowing!

The other day, we went to three infirmaries of brothers who were sleeping in nightmares. It's sad to see them. Some keep their eyes open and still. Most don't speak; their faces are of horror. They were all cleaned and well settled and yet pleasant to look at. They keep the images of their mistakes running through their minds, repeatedly. Sometimes they groan in anguish. We carefully cared for them, cleaned them, settled them, gave them passes and offered prayers. Many later calmed down, their expressions improving. The length of time they stay this way is varied, some stay for years,

Live in the Spirit World

others for months. When they wake up, they move to another ward. The sick keep changing words until they recover. When they recover, they choose what to do: they start working at the Station, or they go to the Colonies to study, or they reincarnate.

In the evening we listened to music. A worker from the Observation Station provided us with lovely songs.

Her name is Cecília, she sings very well, she has a beautiful voice. Good music helps to restore energy. It is always nice to listen to songs in the company of friends: the workers of the Observation Station love to receive these excursions and visits, they like to talk, to exchange information. The evening went smoothly.

5.– SAMARITANS

The next day, right after the morning prayer, the alarm was raised. The Samaritans were approaching. We stayed in the courtyard to wait for them. The door was opened, and they came in.

They came in vehicles that are impossible to describe. They cannot convey identical situations, because they aren't the same on the two planes of life. I can only transmit similarities of psychic and spiritual states. spiritual states. There may be visual similarities, but not identical facts in external and internal content. We stayed to observe them, except Joaquim, who went to help them. Samaritans are the workers of the Station that go out into the Samaritans are the workers of the Station, who go out into the Doorway to help those who want help. They were dressed, for better work, in high boots and capes with beige to light brown caps. Like the ones we use to cross the doorway. The rescued were half naked, and the few dressed had their clothes dirty and in rags. We felt sorry for them. They were dirty, with long hair and fingernails. Some spoke, others remained as mummies, not moving, although with their They did not move, although their eyes were open and terrified. Many groaned sadly. For an instant, I was saddened. Seeing those brothers like that was touching. I never thought I would see so much

Live in the Spirit World

suffering. Many showed signs of torture. We remained silent, it seemed that for a moment we didn't feel like talking to speak, the scene moved us.

A rescued woman, when she saw one of the workers, exclaimed, "An angel! You are an angel! Help me, for God's sake!

Then they would be sent to the wards and separated, depending on their condition.

- Please let me keep her!

A man was holding the hand of a woman, who was sleeping in a nightmare.

- I'll arrange for them to be together. - Thank you! - replied a Samaritan.

Guillermo confirmed the request. They would be together. Usually, because of their states, they would be separated. However, these two were united and the man, in a better state, cared for the woman, in a worse condition. It was clear that they loved each other. " I'm glad they were together" - I thought.

The group of Samaritans consisted of two women and six men. They greeted us smiling and went to guard the vehicles. Afterwards, these workers would eat and rest. We approached each other, admiring their courage and disinterest. I asked one of them:

- Do you like this job? How long have you been doing this?

- I love going in search of those who ask for help in the name of God. I was rescued by a caravan like this, fifteen

Live in the Spirit World

years ago, in this Station, and for five years I have been in this job.

- How do you feel, being a woman, in a job that requires so much courage? - Our distraught Zé asked one of the workers, a girl in her thirties and very pretty.

- There isn't work on the spiritual plane only for men or women. Here we're God's creatures. I like what I do. Every time I return to the Station with suffering brothers and sisters, it brings joy to my heart.

The caravan brought twenty-one helpers. These workers stay for days at the Doorway, going to all the places where they are needed and always helping many brothers.

The length of stay at the Station varies from two to three days. During that time, they make plans, design routes for the next help.

Soon after the rescuers were picked up, the tower sounded the alarm.

The sound of the alarm is a soft chime. There are four ways of sounding the alarm. Three short ones, as given to the Samaritans, signify the approach of diligence for good. A soft, long ringing signifies the approach of ignorant brethren.

Another louder ringtone is used to warn about attacks; which has a different sound, warns that the Station is about to be attacked by many spirits. Even if there isn't a scandal and all is silent, the sound reaches people who need to be alerted. The bell doesn't ring in the halls.

The tower guard told us that a group of ten brothers of darkness is approaching.

Live in the Spirit World

- Let's wait and see what they want - said Guillermo. Again, the watchman said that the group had stopped a few meters away. Soon we heard screams.

- What are they shouting? - Luíza asked. Are they saying Valeria?

- I think it's Venancio - said James.

One of the rescuers came out of the playground in desperation.

- It's him! It is Valencio! - explained a Samaritan.

The man was in a horrible condition, he had been tortured and was severely bruised, signs of torture marked his entire body. Guillermo and one of the workers held him and took him back inside.

Frederico explained:

- This rescued man was being tortured by that group. He repented and asked, in time, for help in the name of God. This time, the rescuers brought him in, and his executioners chased him. Now they will take him to a chamber where he won't hear those calls.

- What did he do to be treated like this? - Gloria asked with pity.

- It's unfortunate for those who do evil, because those who receive them don't always forgive. There comes a day when death makes them meet. Indeed, they tortured him for revenge - Frederico said.

- If they shouted my name, would I, like him, be desperate? - I was impressed. Frederico smiled and said:

Live in the Spirit World

- Certainly, no. You haven't ties to them. To feel their calls, it's necessary to be linked to them, to have the same vibrations and to have stayed a long time, as this brother stayed with them. If a group were to call you, you simply wouldn't listen. You need not fear.

The fear is for those who doubt.

The watchman in the tower was alert, but those in the group shouted from a distance for thirty minutes. When they failed, they decided to leave.

- What if they attacked? - Luíza asked, worried.

- We would have to defend ourselves with electric beams - answered Guillermo calmly.

- "Does it always happen what we witnessed here? - Ivo asked.

- Yes. Sometimes they resign themselves to losing their victims. Some, like these, simply call them, others attack us. But, once inside, no one leaves without leaving - answered Guillermo.

It was eleven o'clock in the morning, time to leave. We parted gladly, as we would return to the Station to study the Doorway. Guillermo thanked us and Raimundo returned our thanks on behalf of everyone. We left through the door and lined up. We would walk to the Charity and Light and then take the airbus that would take us back to Colony.

It was cold at the Doorway, but we did not notice. As I said, we had learned to neutralize the outside temperature. But I felt a bit suffocated. I stayed very close to Blue Flower, who was still quiet. I confess that the Doorway scares me.

Live in the Spirit World

Reading or seeing it in movies is one thing, but there, personally, it is another. Nothing is beautiful or pleasant. We returned without problems. When we arrived at the Charity and Light Shelter, it was a relief. We only stopped there to take the airbus. I was tired, and the shuttle arrived at a good time.

How nice to be in the Colony! We arrived in the evening and went straight to our accommodations, where we ate and rested. I liked to write down everything I could, and it was during those hours of rest that I did so. After writing it down, I slept for a few hours.

Early the next day we had the concluding class. The questions were many.

- Do the workers at the Stations get overtime, and do the Samaritans earn more? - Cecilia asked.

- It's easy to learn. I studied the subject in the food course on how to feed myself that I took in the Colony and transcribed it in the book Violets on the Window; the disincarnate person who doesn't know how to neutralize the outside temperature feels hot and cold.

Raimundo was chosen to answer:

- Working hours are counted for everyone. Hourly bonuses are given to those who want and need them. In work that requires more effort and expends more energy, they're doubled and sometimes tripled, like that of the Samaritans.

- Are the Samaritans attacked? - Gloria asked.

- These workers are called in many ways: missionaries, emissaries, etc. They are often attacked many times. They

Live in the Spirit World

always leave the regions of the Doorway and sometimes stay at the Station only for hours. Rare is the excursion when they are not attacked. Our friends are not intimidated by this. They have protective nets and are always equipped with lightning launchers, small defense devices. They're smart and always do well, because they aren't in the mood for fights and therefore command respect.

- They are heroes! What a tough job! I admire them. Do they get time off? - Marcela spoke excitedly.

- Yes, they have free time off and spend it as they please, some come to the Colony, some visit friends and others stay at the Station.

- Do they travel through the Doorway? - I asked.

- Yes, they do. On each excursion they go to one part of the Doorway. They go into all the caves, holes, valleys, in short, everywhere. They are experienced and know all the Doorway places in this region.

- Do they also go to the Doorway cities? asked James.

- Yes, they do. Sometimes they ask permission to pick up people who want help. Other times, the inhabitants of the cities of the Doorway see the Samaritans helping some brothers. When those brothers are not in the interest of those who live there, the Samaritans work without problems. However, when they want to help someone who is in the interest of the residents of the Doorway, the Samaritans enter unseen. As in the case of the tortured man we saw who was called by the gang, outside the wall.

Live in the Spirit World

- Are there rescuers around the Doorway, all over the world? - Cida asked.

- Yes, there are rescuers working in the name of Jesus the Doorway all over the Earth, helping all those who suffer and cry out for help.

- Have these rescuers never been arrested? Have not ignorant spirits who, like the Doorway, would never arrest some of them? - Nair asked.

- We have had no news of this happening. In a larger attack, they can change the vibration and become invisible to others.

I mumbled under my breath and Raimundo told me:

- Patricia, do you want to say something?

- I am thinking: I would not want to work in an Aid Station at the Doorway, I don't think I have the conditions. But I admire those who work there.

- These jobs require people with a lot of love and charity. That's why we should respect workers and admire what they do.

We all looked at Joaquim, who was a little embarrassed: those we saw in the Station rooms take time to improve? - Cida asked curiously.

- It depends a lot on each one. There are brothers who take years to improve, but others do it in months.

- Are there any rescuers who don't like the Station? - Ivo asked.

Live in the Spirit World

- Yes, there are, although those who are taken there want help, because they are almost always tired of suffering. We cannot accept unrepentant brothers who don't want help, because they think everything is bad.

Others say that in the stations there is too much discipline and they want to leave. Some spirits who have not suffered enough and are housed in the Aid Stations, at the request of third parties or by teams working in Spirits centers, often don't like it and don't stay, they return to their homes and wander.

- I -said Rosalia -, I went to the Observation as a rescued person. I am grateful to everyone. But seeing the Station as an apprentice is different.

- Of course, it's. She was sick, in need, and knew the parts where she lived. Now, she went to meet him as a student, and everything seemed different.

- Rosalia, do you remember anything about when you were there as a rescued person? - asked Zé.

- Yes, how can we forget the suffering? I was a human rag, it was painful. Remorse is a burning fire.

As there were no more questions, Raimundo said:

- Do an essay, write what you saw, what impressed you most.

It is not compulsory work. Only those who want to do the essay do it. Those who have difficulty writing and prefer to talk will tell how they felt and what they liked. Some prefer to just listen.

Live in the Spirit World

The fifteen would read what they wrote. Everyone would talk about the Samaritans. We exchanged ideas. Ivo and Luis said that, after the course, they will work in a Station at the Doorway.

Getting to know these stations, these places of peace amid suffering, was gratifying. They are blessed houses of help. They are a refreshment for the tormented brethren.

How good it is that there are such places and how wonderful that there are good workers of good in them!

6.- DISINCARNATION

At the beginning of the theory class, we began by narrating our own reincarnations. Everyone, in fact, has an interesting story to tell. Nobody had the disembodiment in the same way, although it is natural and for everyone.

I narrated mine, in a few words:

- I was reincarnated by a cerebral aneurysm, I did not see or perceive anything; for me it was like sleeping and waking up among friends. I adapted quickly, I was a Spirits, and this fact helped me a lot.

- You came with a diploma! - exclaimed Ivo playfully. You knew what was going to happen to you and what you were going to find. You are very clever!

- In fact - I answered - Who has religion inside and lives according to the Gospel is intelligent!

Spiritism is well understood and educates for the continuation of life.

- Do you think, Patricia, that, as you were a Spirits, you had and received a lot here in the Spiritual World? - Zé asked, referring also to the fact that Blue Flower accompanied us on the excursions because of me.

Live in the Spirit World

- Zé, Spiritism has provided me with a favorable environment to realize myself internally.

I followed the Doctrine of Allan Kardec, I lived the Gospel of Jesus.

Mrs. Isaura gently interrupted:

- Patricia is well suited to one of the teachings of The Gospel According to Spiritism, Chapter XVIII - Many are called, and few are chosen. In section twelve, which tells us: "Therefore, much will be asked of the spiritists, because they received much, but also to those who knew how to take advantage of the teachings, much will be given".

Zé recounted his disincarnation:

- My disincarnation was great, it's to die laughing. I was scared to death, It's true! I was fine, at least I didn't feel anything. One day, a friend and I went for a drive. As we crossed the train line, the car stopped, broke down and wouldn't start. Just then the train was approaching. My friend ran out of the car. Desperation made me stand still. My friend yelled at me to get out, and when I wouldn't do it, he came back and tried to get the car to start, until he succeeded, and left a second before the train passed.

" That scared me, eh, Zé!'

"No answer. My heart just stopped, making me die instantly. I only heard my friend speak, then I lost consciousness. My spirit fell asleep. I woke up alone, I was lying near the train line. I did not feel anything, so I got up and went home. When I got there, I found myself crying. I

Live in the Spirit World

went inside and had another scare. I found myself in the coffin. I was feeling sick and no one cared.

Confused, I was thinking, "Did I die? Did I go crazy? Did another guy who looked like me die?" But nobody saw me. I decided to cry out. In the moment of oppression, as always, people turn to God. I started shouting to God, asking for forgiveness and help. I was shocked. "Calm down, Zé, such scandal!" It was my mother who had been gone for a long time. "Mother - I shouted -, help me! Have I died or am I crazy?" "Calm down, son, try to calm down. Are you a ghost?" I asked more calmly. "No, I'm your mother, who loves you very much. Don't be afraid, I will help you." Mom took me to a corner of the house where there was no one and returned to the living room, where the coffin with my body was, to finish disconnecting me. Two friends walked by me and commented: "Zé must be telling jokes to Saint Peter". The other replied: "He died of fear, is this a way to die? Jokes to Saint Peter" - I thought – "I am going through a serious problem". Then, a group of women began to pray, I felt better and calmer, I gradually felt sleepy. Come on, Zé! - said Mom. I settled in her arms and slept. I woke up and thought I had been dreaming, but later I realized it was all true. I was always very cheerful and a church-going Catholic. I accepted the fact well and tried to get used to the new life: soon I was working and now today I take this course to serve better.

- I was once an atheist! - Ivo began. An atheist convinced me that I was right. I thought, when I was incarnated, that everything was by chance. God was a personality invented to terrorize the ignorant. There was nothing but the death of the body. I became ill, a serious

Live in the Spirit World

illness that bedridden me; then, at times, I asked myself, "Am I right?" I became afraid, and I thought that the illness was what frightened me. The idea of suicide occurred to me, but I repelled it, I wasn't a coward, I could bear the suffering. I decided to wait until the end.

Not believing in anything is sad, there's no consolation and, thinking that we're finished, it gives a feeling of agony.

"I did not notice my disincarnation. I continued to act like a sick person in the hospital for a long time, feeling the abandonment of my family. Afterwards, the playful spirits took me out of the hospital and brought me to the cemetery. They told me I had died, that I had disincarnated, but I could not understand anything. I didn't know how to pray, the little Gospel I knew not coming to mind, because I had never paid attention to it. In the incarnate, I laughed at religious people, but I wasn't evil. If I didn't do good, neither did I do evil. I was taken to a city of the Doorway, as a slave. I had to do certain kinds of jobs for them. For years I was like that, until I understood everything: life continues after the death of the body and God exists. Because I was tired of suffering, I turned to this God in whom I did not believe, and who is our Loving Father.

I was not helped immediately, but I did not give up, and every day, with more faith, I asked for help. I was rescued, taken to a Station. I recovered, grateful and eager to get better, and I became useful. I stayed a long time at the Station. Then I came to the Colony to work. I often changed the way I worked many times, get to know what it's like to live here. Having won praise for my work, because I was

Live in the Spirit World

never lazy, and forced labor as a slave is very painful, but one learns to work, so I requested to study.

I think that, if I get to know this wonderful world, I can become more securely established in my faith and useful.

I died forty-five years ago, twenty-five years I have suffered wandering and in the Doorway. Twenty-five years is a lot, but it was fair. Who doesn't believe everything, is only awakened by suffering."

Ivo - Luíza asked -, if you had been bad, would you have suffered more?

- Certainly yes, I think more and for a longer time.

Teresita spoke of her disincarnation. She is quiet, soft-spoken, very friendly:

- I was very religious, I loved to pray a lot, but unfortunately religion didn't teach me what death would be like. I had a spreading cancer, which caused me a lot of suffering.

So, I asked myself: "Why do I suffer so much? Is God unjust to me?" I tried to strengthen my faith, but I didn't understand, and faith without reason is difficult to maintain. I was reincarnated and was taken to a Station. I got better soon, but I thought I was still incarnated and was healing. When I was told I was disincarnated, I didn't believe it; then, as I thought and analyzed, I was terribly disappointed that I wasn't as I thought and became apathetic. I wanted nothing, I did not want to listen to anyone, and I thought again, "What was the use of having been good and devoted? Was God just being me?" The Station supervisors will take me to a Spirits

Live in the Spirit World

meeting. At the Center, I saw many maimed and suffering and heard the counselor: "Do you see how good it was to be good and devoted? I watch that many, with their dead bodies, didn't have a cure like you, and were not taken to an Aid Station." I was looking at everything with curiosity, I didn't join in, I just listened and came back differently. Many times, I went to meetings and, together with the counselors, I went to meet the Doorway. I got better, I came out of apathy and I knew that my disincarnation with suffering was to solve the mistakes of the past.

The spiritual world fascinated me, and I became a helper; today I have the grace to learn to serve more wisely.

Ilda, with simplicity, narrated her disincarnation:

- I was very happy, was married to the man I loved, and my house was a dream. When I got pregnant I was the happiest woman. My childbirth was complicated, and I was reincarnated after having a baby girl. I was rescued and taken, after the death of my body, to an Aid Station. How I suffered so much. I tried hard not to rebel. I could feel the cries of my parents and my husband. It's not easy to leave everything when you're happy, it's not easy; only if we have understanding, such as Patricia, who was also happy and remained so. My parents took the baby girl, my daughter to raise her, and my husband went back to his parents' house. I was missing them so much, I wanted to take care, cuddle, hold and breastfeed my daughter, I wanted to be incarnated! Just thinking about them, I didn't pay attention to anything else. I had to receive indoctrination, through incorporation, in a Spirits Center, and have a treatment with a psychologist

Live in the Spirit World

here. Little by little I got used to it. My husband has remarried and has other children. My daughter is already a teenager.

Now I love to live here, but it was not easy. All I went through was a difficult but necessary learning process for my spirit.

Disincarnation is the birth of the spirit into the spirit world. We had a lesson in anatomy. We studied the strengths and watched movies on how to disconnect the perispirit from the corpse. The rescue teams that perform this disengagement usually meet in groups of three to four rescuers. For working in this process, they do a long study and training, and they can only do the immediate disconnection of a few people. That's why there are not many of these tasks. We saw them at work in movies, when they did several disengagements.

After this course, any of us could disengage someone after their body died, but we should not do it without a superior order. It's good to know! To know is to be able to do it!

The disconnection is done in various ways, it can be minutes after the death of the body, a few days or months. It depends on the merit of the disincarnate.

We studied a lot of the part of the human body and using dolls, we watched how the disengagement takes place. These dolls are faithful copies of the human body and the perispirit.

We understood perfectly how the physical body works, what happens to it and how it disintegrates.

Live in the Spirit World

I was impressed to see, in movies, the disconnection of people who commit suicide. That always takes place a long time after the reincarnating. It's sad! The worst reincarnating, although each case is different. Those who practice this crime against themselves suffer a lot.

The theoretical class was very good, and I was looking forward to the practical class.

7.- DISENGAGEMENT

The practical classes were very important. Blue Flower joined us, as always, very kind and worked hard. First, we went to hospitals in the region. As much as we study, seeing the task personally is different, because, sometimes, emotion and piety come in. Moreover, because it's with the disincarnation that we find the friends or enemies we made when we incarnated. First, we saw the reincarnation of a man whom the rescue team came to disengage. Many friends and family members were waiting for him.

He disincarnated calmly. It was beautiful, but soon afterwards we saw the reincarnation of another man, whom many obsessors were waiting for. We prayed for him, but we could not prevent the obsessors from unlinking him and took him, certainly, to the Doorway.

Mrs. Isaura took the opportunity to enlighten us:

- We are here for learning, in helping all those who were entitled to help from the good. We cannot interfere with anyone's harvest. This gentleman has vibrated with those below him and not with us; all his life he has been in tune with them, with these dark brothers, and now he can only have the company he himself chose. By making mistakes, we

Live in the Spirit World

are vibrating with the wrong ones. This gentleman needs to suffer to learn. Suffering is the medicine he needs.

We saw many reincarnations. In the big hospitals there are many. We helped the rescuers, many of them.

Wherever we went, we would introduce ourselves, upon arrival, to the people in charge of the place. We were always well received and have been to many hospitals.

Children's discharges are quick. Usually, when they are about to disincarnate, a team of rescuers is already nearby, and they always take them to an Aid Station.

I was impressed because children always move me, but it is easier, they are not usually as attached to the subject as adults.

Afterward, we were on duty on the busiest highways. On the large highways, there are, at specific points, small Aid Stations and, in the simplest accident, a device is activated that indicates the location and the severity. The rescue team arrives even before the material rescue. The workers greeted us with joy. I had hoped there would be nothing, but there were several accidents. The roadside Aid Stations are always in contact, so when an accident occurred, we were informed instantly and immediately went to the scene. It is not nice to see people hurt and in pain. We help both the injured and the disincarnated. Disengagement in accidents is sometimes violent, as the body dies, and the peri spirit is instantly extinguished. We take many spirits to the roadside Aid Station. There they receive first aid, then they are taken to other Aid Stations.

Live in the Spirit World

Sometimes we just disconnect without helping the spirit. There are disengagements that take a short time. Others take hours.

After many hours on the highways, where we've seen many accidents with deaths and many injuries, we went to the cemetery.

- Here there are many attached physical bodies, our learning work is to help, to detach as many as we can.

There were many who grunted next to the rotting bodies; others slept in nightmares. The rescue workers from the cemetery came to greet us:

- Welcome, students! We are very grateful for your presence. Whenever you come here, you succeed in helping many brothers and sisters who did not know how to disincarnate and suffer.

The wandering spirits, troublemakers, like to wander in the cemeteries, mess with those who are suffering and laugh at those who think they're incarnated. We were warned to ignore them. During our work, they watched us, even made fun of us, but without approaching.

In the cemetery, there were many people attached to the dead body.

- There are so many! - exclaimed Zé - I bet we can take half of them to the rescue. I bet there will only be ten - said Luís.

- Three are left - I said.

The group is happy, you cannot lower the vibe with sadness and pity without help. We talked for fun.

Live in the Spirit World

We wanted one to be left without help. I repeat that we could only help those who asked with humility, sincerity and those who needed help, but not the rebels who blasphemed. These are very needy, but it is useless to take them to a Station, because they don't accept and only bring problems to the place where they are taken.

So off we went, enthusiastic, to try to talk to them, it is not easy!

We passed them around, mentalizing our strength to see if we could wake them up, calm them down and get them to think about Jesus, about God. Three sleeping ones woke up terrified and, as soon as we dislodged them, they ran away.

No doubt they would be rescued later. The moaning ones were upset by the pain and horror of being there. We gave them a pass and asked them to stay calm. We were able to disengage many, helping them and taking them to the Aid Station. In almost every cemetery there is a small Aid Station, where the first responders take the rescued, for a short time.

Some repelled our help, even cursing us. We could do nothing for them.

This is delicate work for me, and I admire those who do it. It is not easy to see so much sadness. I wanted to help them all, but it was not possible, and so many were trapped there in their decomposing bodies. But our work was worth it, because the few we helped filled us with joy.

I admire the first responders at the cemeteries.

Live in the Spirit World

Almost everyone lives in the small Station, works hard, have little time off and are happy. They love their love doing what they do.

- I had imagined that I would get dirty dealing with so many dirty brothers, some even rotting - Luíza said sincerely.

Frederico answered:

- No, Luíza, we do not get dirty. Afterwards, we know how to mold cleanliness, to clean ourselves by the power of the mind. In fact, most of the suffering brothers here are dirty, but we must look at the suffering brothers and sisters who suffer and think that perhaps we could be one of them. Outside dirt is not an obstacle to help.

We went to see some funeral ceremonies. Always a gray cloud of sorrow and agony hangs over the place.

We saw some where only the body was veiled, with the spirit already disconnected, body absent.

But in some funerals the spirit was there, confused. In others, they slept near the body. The only thing that gets in the way is crying. It would be good if everyone was good. It would be if everyone understood disincarnation as it is and accepted this physical absence, helping the disincarnated with thoughts of affection, praying with faith, helping them to disengage in their journey to the spiritual plane.

Raimundo went with Joaquim to deal with a case in another place. We had two hours to stay in the bark and do whatever we wanted. Almost everybody followed Mrs. Isaura, who wanted to return to the cemetery. It was night

Live in the Spirit World

and I invited the group to go to my earthly home. Some accepted, Frederico accompanied us. There were seven of us.

After entering the house and settling in the TV room. I always get excited when I enter my old house. It's very nice to feel the fluids of the family members, the human warmth, the affection with which they remember me.

We began to talk. My family was sleeping.

The conversation became heated, Zé ended up making physical noise on the TV. We were immediately silent. Then my parents woke up and went to see what had caused the noise. Seeing nothing, they soon went back to sleep. Zé, he was serious:

- Respect Patricia's house, you half-assed haunt we laughed.

Zé used to say that we are not overly fancy and not that important. We are nothing more than half...

Frederico explained to us that it was possible to make the noise because there was someone sensitive at home and because we were in our conversation. He politely asked Zé not to make this kind of joke anymore. Zé understood and apologized.

We got on the airbus at the appointed time, which was at an Aid Station, and returned to the Colony. In the concluding class, we all wanted to talk. The first responders in the cemeteries were our heroes.

- I wanted to disengage everyone I saw, even if they were connected to the corpse - said Teresita. Could we not have done that?

Live in the Spirit World

- If we had unlinked everyone, we would not have acted prudently - answered Mrs. Isaura -. When we do something prematurely, it almost always harms the rescue. All patients need the right medication.

- We have also seen family members disengaging their loved ones, without the presence of rescuers. I did not think it was possible - said Marcela.

- You know now, and those who know can do it, if they have permission. You have seen relatives disengaging their family members, but only those who could already be helped; the others those who have no merit, the relatives cannot help.

- We saw the obsessors turn off that man. I thought only the good ones knew about it - Luis said

- Knowing is not only the privilege of good people. The bad ones know it and more. Yes, they disengage, and they do it with partners and with those they hate.

- Can evil spirits make a person disincarnate? - Ivo asked.

- No. Neither an evil spirit or even a good spirit can do it. They can only disengage. And they disengage when the body is already dead. The death of the body follows the law of nature. An incarnate can kill another incarnate. But the disincarnate can't kill the body of an incarnate. Both the good and the bad must wait for the physical body to die to detach the perispirit.

- We have been disincarnated so many times, and each time it seems phenomenal. Why is that? - Gloria asked.

Live in the Spirit World

- There is a lack of education about disincarnation, and a lack of understanding. Among the incarnate, it's Spiritism that provides an understanding of disincarnation. Moreover, it's not always lived in incarnation as it should be, death, unknown to many, ends up causing panic.

-Are there people who know disincarnation well and manage to disengage themselves? - I asked.

- These are rare cases, but they do. Who knows, it does.

That made me doubly happy, I thought of my family; surely, if they continued to study as they do, they would not be attached to the corpse, and then, now I knew, I learned to help.

The disengagement was really an interesting theme!

8.- REINCARNATION

In the theoretical class, we studied anatomy and the human body. Then we saw, through movies, many reincarnations. We witnessed twin births, observing how two or more spirits prepare to reincarnate together. Also, how the process of forgetting the past is done. We do not want to start remembering the past. We have the blessing of forgetting our mistakes, so that in the new body we can start again without the pain of remorse.

- It's useful to remember the past, the other existences? - Teresita asked.

- When disincarnate, only those who can do so remember, and if it is useful for them. In the case of the incarnated, only in some. It's harmful to remember out of curiosity. Sometimes, remembering is a therapy. As in people with a tendency to suicide. Perhaps by knowing a little of what he suffered when he committed suicide in the past life, he will fight against this tendency and try to overcome it. Some people with trauma have their problems eased by remembering. When one remembers for himself it's because he is mature enough for that. On the contrary, when immature spirits get too many memories, they go crazy - Raimundo answered.

Live in the Spirit World

- When I was incarnated, I saw crazy people, who had two personalities, did they remember the past? - Ivo asked.

- Each case must be analyzed to make a diagnosis. But it may be that, remembering without the proper preparation, the physical brain gets sick, confusing everything. I know of obsessors who, seeing that the incarnate tends to madness, force him to remember the past and, therefore, he becomes ill. Forgetting is a blessing!

- But we have facts of the past, fears, affections and disaffections left in us, right? Always, when you incarnate, you have the feeling of knowing places or people - said Rosalia.

- We all forget the past when we reincarnate, but the impression of the most remarkable events remains in many. That is why we feel those sensations.

Many interesting facts were told. There are groups that are in tune with a large spiritual family and always seek to reincarnate together, helping each other. There is also reincarnation to reconcile spirits, although this is not always achieved. We know of so many cases like this, members of a family hating each other and sometimes even killing each other.

Joaquim recounted his story:

- Enemies for centuries were another spirit and me. In my last existence we were reincarnated as brothers so that we could learn to love. Since we were little we fought, hating each other. During one of these fights, he severely wounded me with a knife and I became disincarnated days later. Fortunately, he repented, asked me to forgive him, and I

Live in the Spirit World

forgave him from the bottom of my heart. He is still incarnated and sincerely repentant. But there were so many offenses between us, we'll have to be together again to unite bonds of affection.

- Will they be able to fight again? - Cecilia asked. Joaquim answered:

- I hope not. I have been working to learn: I work at the Station, at the Doorway, amid much suffering to realize the good. To love everyone as myself.

We went to the Colony's Reincarnation Department. It is a very nice building, surrounded by gardens. The building of three floors is only for the Department. Countless people work there. It's simply decorated with light beige paint. It has many offices. First, we stayed in the lobby where there were several people preparing for reincarnation. We mingled with them, chatting to learn about their problems and what they wanted.

I approached two women and introduced myself. The older one said:

- I am here to ask for reincarnation. My great-granddaughter, a very dear spirit, wants to get pregnant, I hope to be that baby. I trust her, and I know she will raise me well.

- I'm worried - said the other madam. I want to reincarnate to forget. I made many mistakes in my past existence and, although I try not to suffer for them, I can't, remorse haunts me. I asked to forget, with the blessing of reincarnation. But I abused addictions, with alcoholic beverages and tobacco, damaging my healthy body. Now,

Live in the Spirit World

when I incarnate, I will have some diseases that will keep me away from such addictions.

I was thinking about what I heard. I looked at Frederico and I asked: Frederico, could what that lady said happen?? - And I told him the fact.

- Patricia, we are what we built in the past and we will be in the future what we built in the present. That woman was not able to educate herself. If she reincarnates in this way, she will be able to transmit to the physical body whatever it thinks.

I mingled with the others again. I approached a man and a woman still young. She said to us:

- I really like the person who will be my father. But I do not like how my mother will be. I know she has no sympathy for me.

- Did you not learn to love her? - I asked

- Well, It's not easy. She is very boring. Again, I went to ask Frederico.

- Now, Patricia, all of us who are on the reincarnation list have faults to overcome and virtues to acquire. It's not because they're going to reincarnate that it means they're saints or that they have learned everything in a manual on how to live well. If they were perfect, the Earth wouldn't be in this mess we see.

The fact is that this preparation is only available to a few. Just as there are also few who can choose their countries, how they will be, among others. This preparation is only

Live in the Spirit World

possible for those who work, are in the Colonies and in the Aid Stations.

There are many halls in the Department. The order room is very popular. It is where requests for reincarnation are made. The people who work in the Department are trained and very well experienced. They have tasks in the Department and on Earth, monitoring reincarnations and helping to raise awareness.

There is the mold hall, where the body shapes that future reincarnations will have been studied. It's very beautiful; we saw some molds of perfect bodies, which would have diseases after a certain age, and others. The technicians are prepared, studious and like what they do. These molds are made like this: the spirit that wants to reincarnate goes there and asks to be molded. Depending on the parent's physique, the technicians draw the model, considering the reincarnates requests, such as diseases, details, etc. When they are reincarnated and their perispirit shrinks to connect with the unborn child, everything is made based on this mold. The mold is made for the unborn child, but you know what it will look like as an adult. Not everyone who reincarnates makes use of this room. Even few can choose the body they will have. These few are the cases, where there are problems, where the Department's scholars ask for them to be made, and the cases of spirits with much merit.

There is also the waiting room, where there are the candidates for reincarnation who ask to be reincarnated and wait their turn.

Live in the Spirit World

I learned a lot by talking to people. And I realized that they don't think the same way. Many like the incarnate life and ask for a new chance in the body. Others wanted reincarnation because it was necessary for them, but they loved the spiritual plane. In some of them fear was present, they were afraid of losing themselves in matters.

They know that incarnation deceives many and that the path of comforts is more pleasant. They know that growing spiritually is not easy.

We talked a lot, we encouraged everyone. Reincarnating is dying to the spiritual world.

The practical class was great, at least we didn't see any crying. Birth is almost always a reason for joy.

Blue Flower joined us. I asked her

- How is the work at the Spiritist Center going?

- Very well. We've had a lot of activities lately. I thought, " That poor boy, so much work and he is here with me."

I forgot he could read my thoughts. He replied calmly:

- Yes, there is a lot of work, but mine is this now and I do it with love. Poor man who doesn't like what he does. Knowing that you trust me to protect you is a gift I receive.

I smiled and thought, "I have a lot to learn, to live without giving a 'problem' on the spiritual plane."

First, we went to see the parents' meeting with their future children. The Department's workers take the spirit, that is, the candidate for reincarnation, to the parent's home or mother.

Live in the Spirit World

They take the incarnate out of the body while they sleep. For the most part these are happy meetings. There are difficulties only when reincarnation and reconciliation take place, since the incarnates don't want to accept their enemies as their children. It's exciting to see like-minded spirits meet again. We are moved to see a reunion between a future father and son.

Two spirits have been friends for centuries.

We've also seen spirits attached to unborn children. The reincarnated spirit stays with the mother, united. It's so nice!

How wonderful motherhood is!

We witnessed a frustrated reincarnation, which didn't work. The pregnant woman fell ill, damaged the unborn child and he died.

- And now what? - Cecilia wanted to know. What is going to happen?

- We'll take the opportunity to help the mother - said Frederico -. This spirit will be taken back to the Department and will try again.

- With this same family? - Ivo asked.

- Everything indicates that yes, because there is affection, but if it's not possible, she will choose another family.

We also watched a mother who arrived at the hospital after causing the abortion and who was bleeding a lot. The reincarnation was stuck to her. The technicians removed him

Live in the Spirit World

from the woman and took it to the Department, to a specific place.

What we enjoyed seeing were the deliveries and helping. How nice it's to see a baby being born. Birth is a celebration for most incarnates. Seeing happy parents with their children is a joy for all of us.

But there are reincarnations that don't work, and the reincarnation of the child happens soon after. This happens for many reasons, and the spirit is always taken back to the Department. There, they plan to reincarnate again or return to their previous appearance to their frustrated reincarnation. This remains as an apprenticeship.

We saw a mother who gave up her son, not wanting to see him. We heard that the reincarnate was her enemy, and that she refused to have him. Again, we went to the classroom for the conclusion. This theme, although fascinating, was not intense. The questions were few.

- How does the spirit feel after an abortion?

- If the abortion was natural, that is, something did not work, and the unborn child died, the reincarnated person feels sorry that it did not work, tries again, sometimes with the same parents; if it's not possible, chooses others. They do not feel pain, nothing. It's as if you are going to take a jump, try and it does not work, then it remains to prepare and try again. In induced abortion, the spirit does not feel pain, but feels repulsion, rejection. Usually, it is rescued and taken to the Department. But there are cases in which the reincarnated rebels cannot be rescued, then it resumes the previous form and becomes an obsessor of the parents or the mother.

Live in the Spirit World

- Could there be any unforeseen accidents in reincarnation? - Ivo asked.

- Yes, we saw a natural miscarriage, in which, unfortunately, the mother became ill and the unborn child died.

- I found very interesting the case we saw of the father who wanted reincarnation for his son, and the mother didn't - commented Cecilia.

- In fact - answered Frederico -, this is common: one spouse wants a spirit for a child, and the other doesn't. Technicians always try to reconcile both parties.

- Do all mothers who give up their children do it because they were their enemies? - Luis asked.

- No, they often do it out of necessity, sometimes because they don't want responsibility. It also happens, as in the case we saw, that they are enemies, and the mother doesn't want it.

There are other types of reincarnation: those not assisted by protective spirits of good. We did not see these cases in the course. Now it's not for me to go into those details, because I'm not yet aware of the subject.

I thought it through, I do not want to reincarnate soon, I love life on the spiritual plane so much! However, I know that someday I will have to do it again. Now I understood what a gentleman in the Department told me:

- Now, if everyone understood what life is like when they are incarnated, they would cry in reincarnation and not in reincarnation!

9.- CAUSE AND EFFECT

The theory class on cause and effect, or causes of suffering, was very busy. Everyone had examples and stories to tell.

Frederico opened the class with a beautiful presentation:

- We are inherited from ourselves. We are whatever we build. If we want to improve ourselves, we must do it now, in the present. In this lesson, we will see people suffering, feel the effect and study the cause. Every cause has an effect. Good causes produce good effects; bad causes produce negative effects. On Earth, few make it to college. For a minority, negative karma is nullified by inner transformation, working for good, and repairing mistakes and making mistakes. It's doing so by suffering. But for the majority, pain eliminates negative karma.

What you paid for is what almost everyone thinks, and it must be so until maturity, for the spirit to understand.

To redeem mistakes, to repair them, a lot of sincerity is needed. Leaving what you must do for the future is postponing; a postponement that isn't always possible, since in the long run the abuse would have worse consequences. It's important to grow with understanding. We all could

Live in the Spirit World

grow through love; if we lose it, pain, a wise companion, comes to drive us. Mending mistakes through love, through inner transformation, is the subject of the Study Colonies, for those who wish to continue learning. So, those who are interested can, after the course, continue studying, deepening in the subject.

"When I was incarnated, I made many mistakes, but I understood the mistake, and this understanding made me work in Medicine with much love." I used my medical knowledge for the good of all who came to me. I exchanged the rescue of suffering for work on behalf of others and for my inner transformation."

On my last visit to Earth, I met Patricia. And she lived incarnated in her penultimate incarnation. This friend made a mistake, suffered and asked to be reincarnated. She planned to disincarnate young after a long illness. However, this wasn't the case. He returned young to the spiritual plane, but he wasn't ill. His experience of goodness, his modification and inner realization overrode the negative karma, and he didn't need to suffer illness to adapt. Modifying the effect, this is possible, but it must be really sincere, and this change, this realization, must be true."

While Frederico was speaking, I felt that it was true, I felt that I would be sick for a long time, always getting worse. This suffering would be a reaction, but it had been modified. I did not have to suffer to overcome it.

Frederico continued explaining:

- The perispiritual body and the material body form a harmonious composition of energies. If we act selfishly, we

Live in the Spirit World

unbalance this vibrant composition in the spirit and body. This leads to decomposition or disease. When the spirit sees the error, it wants to repair it, and, for that, it must change its way of life, not externally, but with a deep understanding. Pain, when understood, transforms the individual in his way of acting. But if he doesn't understand, the pain can induce him to rebel, and there can be a greater accumulation of imbalance or debt.

Frederico paused; we were all paying attention to what he was saying. Wisely he completed:

- The reactions, the effects, can be for happiness as well as for suffering. A person who has lived in goodness must soon disincarnate a reaction of help, of happiness on the spiritual plane.

"The effects of good, which bring peace and harmony, don't need to be modified. Those who suffer, on the other hand, can, through free will and volition, mitigate or nullify it. But our study is about the effects of pain, of suffering."

We could all speak up, give opinions and tell our own story. Murilo was the first:

- When I was incarnated, I had my right arm and hand always with wounds. When it dried up, my arm would turn black. It hurt a lot. I suffered with that, from childhood until my reincarnation. It was only after some time after I was rescued and admitted to a hospital in the Colony, I was cured. Not long ago I was able to find out the reason for my illness, which nothing and no one could cure. In my other existence I was a proud colonel and whipped several black slaves for

Live in the Spirit World

being lazy. I was disincarnated, suffered a lot and blamed the arm and hand that held the whip.

I reincarnated feeling guilty and a disease came to burn the negative fluids that I generated myself through remorse.

Lauro also told his story:

- When I was incarnated, since I was little I had asthma; throughout my existence I had several crises, which afflicted me a lot and I suffered.

I was poor, my parents disincarnated, and I had to work to support myself, since my siblings, also poor, could not take care of me or support me. The crises made me miss work and I was often dismissed. I was very short of breath; when I was very sick, I was admitted to hospital, and it was on one of those occasions that I disincarnated, being buried as a pauper. But I resigned myself, I felt that my suffering was deserved. Many times, I cried, but I did not rebel. I disincarnated and was helped, because all those who suffer with resignation, like me, have the blessing of help in case the person was good. I had to stay in a hospital to eliminate the effect of the disease that was affecting me. Some time ago I learned that I was suicidal in my previous existence. For a foolish reason, I damaged my perfect body, destroying it recklessly. I committed suicide over unrequited love. I threw myself into a deep river, drowning.

Lauro became emotional as he told the story. Mrs. Isaura took the opportunity to clarify some things:

Live in the Spirit World

- Not all reactions, effects, have similar causes. Not all people with asthma acted as Lauro did. There are many reasons for having an existence with difficulty breathing.

Laís also wanted to talk:

- Incarnate, I was married to a good person. I tried everything to have children and I could not. I had lived frustrated and anxious to be a mother. After some time, disincarnated, wanting to know why I did not have children, I learned that in the previous existence I had many abortions, only because I did not want to deform my body. My couple was also the same in that existence and encouraged me to have an abortion.

- Laís - asked Nair -, did you pay for the negative karma you generated? Do you feel at peace about it?

- I suffered and learned through pain to value motherhood. But I could have adopted orphaned children. If I had done that, I would have canceled out of love the negative effect I created. Perhaps, in this very incarnation, I would have had children.

When we love other people's children as our own, we are changing the reaction. Unfortunately, I did not know how to do it.

I was selfish

James recounted what happened to him:

- When I was forty years old, I became deaf. It is very sad not to hear anything. Thirty years ago, I did not hear any sound. I also suffered a stroke that made me bedridden for years. I had many sons, but only one daughter took care of

Live in the Spirit World

me. In this incarnation I was good, honest and hardworking. I believe, or I am sure, that I suffered the mistakes of other existences. But I did not have the courage to remember. Maybe because I did not pay for everything. That is why I study, I want to pay the rest, to cancel the effects of my mistakes, to commit myself to good work, to my inner transformation.

We're all engaged in stories of this kind. Almost everyone talked about themselves, like Gloria:

- I fell ill as a teenager, having seizures, blackouts, struggling and drooled. I suffered a lot, I was constantly embarrassed to give shows. It was enough just to go out of the house to have those attacks. I would go out, I would get nervous and they would come. I was very catholic. I often had these breakdowns during masses, and the pastor would tell me, trying to be nice, that I was excused from going to mass. But I loved going, I loved praying and I was very sad. People were afraid of contagion, and many times I fell in the street and stayed there. We were poor, but if I had a mother incarnate, I was protected. When she passed away, I stayed with my siblings, each season with one. I felt I was not well accepted. But I had nowhere to go, and because of my poor education, I wasn't able to find a job. I was forty years old when I started taking stronger and more modern medications, and the attacks diminished. Disincarnate I was rescued because I suffered with resignation and did nothing wrong. I knew that I lived the first years of being obsessed. And that it was my disincarnated mother who did everything possible to have me forgiven. In my previous existence, I had been a wealthy slave Lord, I committed many evils and I

Live in the Spirit World

wasn't forgiven by three spirits, who accompanied me, taking revenge. After years, they got tired of me because, by praying all the time, I managed to stop them from hitting me too much. But, because of my own mistakes, I suffered.

Today these three spirits are incarnated, and I help them whenever I can. Luíza said:

- During my last incarnation, I had an illness that made me have defective legs. I walked with difficulty.

When I was disincarnated, I came to know that in the previous existence I committed suicide, throwing myself over a precipice, damaging my perfect body.

Mrs. Isaura said again that reactions aren't always the same, although actions always result in a reaction.

Raimundo gave an interesting lesson on how the reaction occurs. When we do wrong, the wrong registers in us. It's like putting your hand on a hot metal, and the pain will come as a reaction either instantly, after months or centuries. But we can, in the time between the act and the reaction, cut that effect or attenuate it with true love, with selfless work for good, and with inner change.

We have watched movies of countries where many people die of hunger, either by drought or war. We have seen the reaction of many people, in similar groups, who need this painful learning to value simple events, fraternity and honesty. Many people felt the effect of the nefarious action of misusing public money. The one who used war to do evil, to accumulate fortunes.

Live in the Spirit World

We also watched people who made many mistakes and marked their perispirits with so many negative fluids that, besides going by affinity to the Doorway and suffering there for years, when they reincarnated they passed these fluids as diseases, to purify themselves.

Not all suffering is due to a negative reaction; sometimes, without taking advantage of the lessons of love to progress, pain forces us to walk. For it's through pain, almost always, that we seek God, a religion, an inner change, and exchange vices for virtues.

The theoretical class was very useful.

10.- ACTION AND REACTION

We did not have much work to do in the practical class; we did everything with little help.

Mrs. Isaura explained:

- I have some records of people incarnated here that I'll take to the crust. We're going to see them, and, from their records, we will know what action provoked the current reaction. Let me make it clear that there is nothing out of curiosity, this is done so that you can learn from true examples.

We arrived on Earth in an airbus, leaving it at an Aid Station. We all went together to see the people we were going to study.

We saw a man in his forties. He was cheerful, mentally handicapped, he spoke feeling very important. Sometimes he walked with his wooden horse, standing on a beautiful horse. He played a toy violin and sang songs that anybody could understand. He would walk through the streets, and some people would help him, others more for fun would antagonize him, making him nervous. Sometimes he would chase people who picked on him. He had epilepsy, which caused him to fall and struggle, leaving him wounded.

Live in the Spirit World

- This brother - said Mrs. Isaura - was obsessed. Over the years, the spirits that accompanied him ended up renouncing revenge. Everything you feel reflects past mistakes. In this incarnation, he is well cared for by the mother, who also suffers from illnesses. They are very poor and go through many needs. In his previous existence, he was a slave lord in this region. He was married, and his ex-wife is now his mother. They were prideful and committed many evils. For maintaining luxury, they left the slaves with almost no clothes and little food. If he used to ride beautiful horses before, now he rides his wooden horse. Once he went to soirees, where he played and sang, while his slaves groaned with suffering, now he is ridiculed as he dances and sings in the streets. His proud spirit learns in a handicapped, unhealthy body, suffering seizures that leave him collapsed in the streets.

We gave passes to him and his mother. This woman in this incarnation suffers with humility. We prayed for them.

Another mute man, also mentally handicapped, was wandering the streets of the city. He was feeling the reaction of a former life as a slanderer and schemer. When he was disincarnated, he had the destructive remorse that damaged his vocal cords and his physical brain. He abused intelligence to harm many people. He was restless, had abdominal pains and we did a prayer circle, he calmed down, was moved and cried. Frederico explained:

- He feels the emanations of affection, because he received our fluids well. May his sufferings be the learning he needs. May he learn to no longer make mistakes.

Live in the Spirit World

They saw a cripple in a wheelchair. This brother rebelled, and the uprising he felt generated dark clouds around him. He was moody and envious. We dispersed the dark clouds with passes and tried to give him optimistic thoughts. The clouds disappeared, but we knew he would soon create them again. We saw his past.

In his previous existence he had been married to a wealthy widow who had a son. His wife had an unmarried brother, who was going to leave his fortune to the nephew who was the best farmhand. The couple had more children, and he wanted his brother-in-law's fortune to go to one of his sons and not to his stepson, as was established. He planned an accident. On learning that his stepson was going to ride a wild horse, he cut the harness and watched. The animal knocked down the young man, who was knocked unconscious. Seeing that he had suffered nothing, he took a stick and broke both of his legs. At that time, there weren't the means available as there are today, and medicine couldn't save his legs. He was crippled and could no longer ride. One of his sons ended up receiving the fortune. And now, in this incarnation, as a boy, he had an accident and his legs were amputated, leaving him in this chair.

- In the uprising, would you rescue your karma? - Ivo wanted to know.

He who rebels does not take suffering as a precious lesson. Sometimes he suffers more, but he rescues. The difference between good suffering and bad suffering is the acceptance and understanding of suffering. By accepting the suffering, when he reincarnates, he is quickly helped; by reincarnating with disgust, he won't have the help, he will

Live in the Spirit World

continue to suffer until he becomes humble - replied Frederico. - Rebellion is bad for oneself. It makes one unpleasant, a person that others don't like to have in their lives. It is bitter, and one suffers more.

We saw a blind couple. Being blind is not easy, just close your eyes and imagine we will be that way for a long time. Each of them had different actions to suffer this reaction. She, out of jealousy, had blinded someone. During her previous existence, she ordered two henchmen to kidnap a young rival, put poison in her eyes and abandon her in the forest. The young woman's eyesight was almost completely damaged. When the criminal mastermind disembodied, she felt remorse, which caused her to go blind; she reincarnated and brought lifeless eyes into the material world.

He is blind and intelligent, he is a spirit who wants to evolve. When he disincarnated, he remembered his past, his previous existences, he saw that a long time ago he was a general who ordered the defeated to be blinded. This shocked him so much that he wanted to return blind to this incarnation, so as not to feel any more remorse. They both work to live, and it's he who supports her with optimism and faith.

- Couldn't he take care of the blind, help them, instead of reincarnating as blind? - Luíza asked.

- It was his choice - answered Raimundo. - We have a free will. Maybe he was afraid of failing. You can make plans to help blind people while disincarnated. Here, incarnated, he changed a lot, because the illusions of matter almost always make us forget our purposes. Lots of people fail.

Live in the Spirit World

Disincarnated, they make many plans, but most return to the spiritual plane broken.

Seeing these people, we gave them passes, cheering them on, making them feel better. We went to visit a school for the mentally handicapped. Many children were there. Three of them were obsessed. First, we surrounded them and made ourselves visible to the obsessors. With delicacy, we tried to convince them to accompany us, leaving their victims. Two of the spirits who were with a girl listened to us attentively, and with relief we heard that they were going with us, as they were tired of suffering and revenge no longer interested them. We took them to the Station of a Spirits Center where, in the next meeting, they would be indoctrinated and taken to a school in the Colony. In the second case, the obsessor looked at us with suspicion, spoke little, promised to think about our proposals and left the place. Obsessed child who was influenced by two spirits. These three were closely intertwined. The obsessors listened to us in a confused way and didn't understand us.

Raimundo said:

- We can do nothing for the moment, but this place is always visited by rescuers, who will pay attention especially to these three, who by common mistakes are intertwined in hatred. Because they remove one of the disembodied, the child runs the risk of disembodiment. She's new to the school, I believe that the first responders will soon be able to guide these disincarnated and take them to a Station.

Many bad deeds that lead spirits to reincarnate with mental deficiencies. It's rare, but there is a spirit that, due to

Live in the Spirit World

a certain objective, reincarnates deficient without the negative reaction. They were spirits who abused intelligence. Others damage the brain with drugs and alcohol. Others committed suicide. Some practiced so many mistakes and destructive remorse caused them to deform the peri spiritual brain, carrying this deformity into the body upon reincarnation.

We approached a child with a very severe disability.

He had been wealthy, the eldest son, and had a sister. He was a teenager when his father passed away, leaving his mother young and very beautiful. When he was seventeen years old, his mother became interested in another man. He started following his mother and heard her talking to her boyfriend. He found out that they were getting married and that she was pregnant. Since he did not want his mother to marry and still have more children to share the inheritance, he planned the crime, killed his mother with a knife, and blamed it on a former slave who worked on the farm. Abolition had already taken place by then. Pretending to be in great pain and indignation, without waiting for a trial, he had the slave put on the log and flogged to death. Also, he insinuated that his mother was the lover of a black man. Then the black man disincarnated on the log with no major problems for him. His grandfather was his legal tutor until he came of age. When he was older, he began to guardianship his younger sister.

He was hardworking, intelligent and multiplied his assets. He didn't want his sister to get married, since she was a young girl, he started giving her drugs, without her realizing it, making her look crazy and sick. The sister

Live in the Spirit World

disincarnated young and became obsessed. He married, had children, was respected, but wound-up taking drugs trying to alleviate remorse. He was reincarnated in a terrible state. The sister haunted him for years. So, the destructive remorse damaged his brain, which was in perfect condition. Reincarnated as you see him now, he centralizes in his body the negative fluids he created.

We look at the disabled with deep love and affection. Their simple smiles, their fragile forms make us want to embrace them. We did that, we gave them joy. Nothing is eternal, and neither is the reaction infinite.

Everything is renewed, time goes by, disincarnate comes, and they, helped and guided, have another reset. I confess that I felt sorry for everyone. Only the imprudent think that there is not return. Watching people suffer the reactions, the effects, is sad. If the incarnate knew that no one does anything without return and that we only cancel these effects with much love and renewal, they wouldn't make so many mistakes.

After hours with them, the excursion ended, and we returned to the Colony. At the concluding class, Raimundo answered many questions.

- Can one be asked to be reincarnated blind, deaf or disabled? - Luíza asked.

- Yes, it can. The Department of Reincarnations studies each case. Applicants receive orientation and, if he wishes, the instructors verify whether it will be good for them or not. Only after a favorable study is done, can he reincarnate with

Live in the Spirit World

a disability, because most of the deficiencies are the ones we create ourselves by our mistakes.

- Can you want to be deficient to grow spiritually, to progress? - Ivo asked.

- Sometimes a spirit thinks that is the only way it will, deficient in material things, he will awaken to progress. But I remind you that disability is a suffering that will only do good to yourself. Progress in the work done for the sake of inner transformation is much more valuable. But there are people who reconcile disability with inner transformation and cope very well. Usually, when this happens, they manage to drag many people along by their example.

- What happens if someone, who suffers a lot from the reaction of his or her bad actions, commits suicide? - Marcela asked.

- In addition, for not paying his negative karma, his situation will also be aggravated. When he commits suicide, he will find worse pain and won't be able to solve his problems.

- I know - said Murilo - a medium who always postpones working for the good, working with his mediumistic. He says it's not yet time to come to work, to follow the Spiritist Doctrine. He has negative karma to cancel. What will happen to him?

- We should not postpone for later what can and should be done today, now. If you must annul your karma and you do not do it, if you lose the opportunity to love, only pain will remain. Making promises isn't enough, you must keep them. I cannot say what will happen to you; perhaps, if

Live in the Spirit World

you continue to refuse to work with mediumship, a wise pain will be a reaction.

- We saw a mentally handicapped man who remembers his past and his mistakes. Other people don't remember, why? - I asked.

- As we've seen, each case is different. You cannot label anything on the Spiritual plane as a rule.

This spirit so fixed his mistakes in his mind, that even with reincarnation he couldn't forget.

- What will happen to him? - I wanted to know.

- He will soon be disincarnated, he will be cared for and admitted to a hospital, in a ward for mentally handicapped brothers, and his recovery will depend on him. Afterwards, as always happens with these brothers, but it's not a rule, I repeat it again, he will reincarnate again and there he will forget everything.

- Do both existences live? - Mauro asked.

- No, he doesn't, he lives what he is today, but his confused mind remembers his past incarnation, aggravating his disability even more. His mind is fixed on the past.

- Do the mentally handicapped are always receive help, when disembodied, by a special team? - James asked

- Yes, it's true. They are disengaged, rescued in their own hospital wards in the Colonies where they recover.

- Are sufferings always reactions? - Gloria asked

- As has already been said, no. When we stop not wanting to progress, pain can push us to progress. There are

Live in the Spirit World

many times when suffering brings us back to the Loving Father, to a religion, to a religion, to an inner change.

This fascinating theme has come to an end; I had a few hours to spare. I went to visit my grandmother and friends. Lenita was waiting for me at school, we hugged lovingly; she went with me to Grandmother's house. It's good to see friends. Grandmother and her friends greeted me with joy. We talked pleasantly. I also went to see my violets, they were beautiful and blooming. How good it's to be loved in this way, to be remembered fondly by loved ones and to receive incentives from them. We were connected by true love, without selfishness. The violets were the symbol of this affection. I kissed their colorful flowers and sent a thought of gratitude to my mother.

I talked enthusiastically about the course and told them details. Grandmother commented:

- Ah, Patricia, if everyone were like you, if all discarnate thought and acted like you!

- Earth would be a planet of regeneration - I said jokingly. I spent pleasant moments with friends.

11.- MADNESS

What is impressive and truly fascinating is the human brain, the central residence of the soul; archive of our past, the birthplace of all human creativity, the seat of all happiness and joy, when there is no conflict.

But most of us do nothing but impair mental capacities through misrepresentation of the forces and energies we receive from divine goodness. It's a commonplace occurrence, one that hardly calls our attention and, when we see it happening with our brethren, we look for the causes of this unhappiness and pain in external agents, such as physical anomalies, or in the ignorance of our obsessive brethren. Hardly do we stop to think that the journey of cosmic nature is towards the perfection of all its manifestations, including man. But man, almost never looks inward and recognizes that it's in himself that the source of his own ills and misfortunes lies.

Meditating on these facts, I began the theoretical class in which we studied the human brain. We saw that the physical brain is identical to the peri spiritual brain. In a difficult class, we studied the parts of the brain and their respective names. We created a "plastic" brain to get a real idea of how it's formed. Impressive and wonderful is the

Live in the Spirit World

human brain. We learned the complicated names of the diseases that affect it and their symptoms.

We've seen movies about mental illnesses also about the sick. We've studied and seen madness without obsession. We would later study the reason why obsession is the cause of many illnesses and madness. Mental illnesses are almost all spiritual origin. They relate to a past full of errors. Many patients remember totally or partially, in a confused way, their previous existences and disturb their brain, which predisposes them to become ill because of the many evils they have committed, they fail in balancing themselves. Memories of the past don't harm balanced people who have already paid their debts or negative karma.

There was an interesting class where we learned to focus on other minds and know what they are thinking or what is happening. We learn to help. You can only read minds with the permission of the person we are investigating, or when they need help. The troubled mind is easy to read, because its thoughts are fixed on a certain subject. Certainly, with these classes alone we wouldn't go out and read thoughts. But it was a start. Developing this process perfectly takes time and practice is necessary. All this study would do is read patients' thoughts and help them. We must focus on the other person's mind, and what he thinks comes to our mind. At first, we read unclear, just pieces, then with training we got better. From discarnate to discarnate is easier. Then I learned to read the minds of the incarnate. However, I only do this for help, never out of curiosity. Then, as I said, the disturbed mind is easier. In mental patients, the thoughts are always very confused.

Live in the Spirit World

In the practical class, we went to the Colony hospital. The disturbed patients stay in the hospital in separate wards.

Depending on these wards they are still isolated, depending on their condition. The rescued ones, of course, were not obsessed, but many had been incarcerated.

We first visited those who were recovering. The infirmary is big, with lots of windows, beds, chairs, some tables with flowers, pictures on the wall and curtains on the windows. It was a women's ward. The patients wear white clothes, dresses or sets of long pants and shirts.

The first impression is that they're well, they are not in pain, but in some, the eyes are somewhat still, in others, restless. Some talk a lot, others are quiet. We were well received; they like to talk and talk about their problems. We have been given guidance and permission to try to put into practice what we learn about mind reading. So, we went there to talk to the patients, try to help them with advice, give passes and invite them to pray with us.

Here I was talking to a girl who looked fifteen years old, but she was twenty-three.

- Do you really want to listen to me? - she asked. Can I tell you about my life?

- Of course, you can. Say whatever you want - I answered.

- I was a good girl, or everyone thought I was. Honest and hardworking, I used to help my mother, a widow, to sew for customers. I behaved a little strange, manic, but nothing serious. I was twenty-two years old, I didn't find a boyfriend

Live in the Spirit World

and ended up falling in love with a married man. We started meeting secretly. I became pregnant. He didn't want to have anything to do with me; he arranged and paid for me to have an abortion. For fear of the bad comments and my mother, I had an abortion. No one found out, but after that action I became ill. I went crazy and was admitted to a sanatorium, where I disincarnated after an electroshock treatment. I suffered a lot, I was persecuted by an enemy spirit from another existence. That spirit, trying to reconcile, was going to be born as my child and I aborted it. It did not forgive me; the hatred became more intense and pursued me through the Doorway. After a while I was rescued. I'm now well.

Observing her, I could see that she had been an indebted spirit who, in her previous incarnation, made many mistakes and, when she disincarnated, she suffered a lot in the Doorway and ended up disturbed. She went through treatment and reincarnated. In the physical life, after a new mistake with the abortion, her brain lost the harmony and the obsessor succeeded in making her sick. If she did not make a mistake in this one, she would not get sick anymore. Thus, we saw cases in which obsessors wait for an opportunity, such as new mistakes and sentimental imbalances, a pain such as the disembodiment of loved ones, which lowers the vibration, to be able to operate.

Sometimes they want to tell us all about it again, they want us to stay close and pay attention to them. The girl grabbed my hand.

- Let me be closer to you, I feel good! Let me! At that moment, no one was in bed. Her name is Isabel, and I was sitting on the chairs near her bed. Some colleagues of mine

Live in the Spirit World

and some patients went out to the courtyard in front of the infirmary, which has many flowered areas. I felt sorry for her and invited her to go with me to talk to a lady who had been looking at us with a smile for a long time. We went, Isabel was quiet, just listening, but she did not let go of my hand. After the greetings, the lady began to speak:

- Daughter, I am sick, but I am not mad as they say. It's funny, here they don't call me mad, but in the other place, yes (she was referring to the incarnation period). I'm a baroness, I talk and talk, and nobody believes me. I have a big, beautiful house, employees and slaves, but live in this ugly house, with people who say they are my relatives.

I must get nice clothes and I dress like this, with the ugly ones. I do not even know who I am anymore. Am I Maria or Carmela? What confusion? Who do you think I am? (She spoke but did not expect an answer.) I am both, or neither. They say I was Carmela, that I died or disincarnated and was born or reincarnated as Maria. But they are all one. Why am I two?

I wanted to be Carmela, who dressed well, ate well, was beautiful and wealthy.

- "Did you not like the black man? - I asked. Maria is black.

- No, I am terrified, they are dirty and stupid. But I am black, don't you see? I was not, and I stayed that way.

I tried to explain that, in the previous existence, she was Carmela, and that her body was dead, then she was reincarnated as Maria.

Live in the Spirit World

She repeated her story again. I gave her a pass and she calmed down. There was a case of remembering out of time, like a green fruit. Perhaps she remembered because of the action of an obsessor, wanting to disturb her. Maybe she herself, fascinated by the incarnation as Carmela, didn't forget, and the memories confused her when she returned as Maria, in an incarnation she didn't like and rejected, because she was poor, ugly and black, a race she detested.

We went to another room. Isabel let go of me in tears and wanted me to promise to see her again. I told her I would do my best. I had little free time and needed to arrange my time off with visitors. When her course was over, I went to see her again. She was feeling much better. She smiled when she saw me, we talked a lot. She had wanted to be reincarnate, she had asked, but the instructors said she had to stay in the Spiritual Plane longer. So, they invited her to study. Isabel is illiterate. I spoke of the school with affection, she was enthusiastic. There she would learn the Gospel, Christian morals, which would do her a lot of good.

These wards we have seen are of patients who, incarnated, had mental abnormalities. In the Spiritual Plane, there are many wards of patients who, incarnated, were healthy and, when they disincarnated, were disturbed by suffering or remorse.

We went to a men's ward. When we entered, a gentleman looked at me and said:

- It's you!

I got scared and Frederico went to him. She what? She is pretty!

Live in the Spirit World

Zé said to me in a low voice:

- That there, Patricia, you are a hit around here!

Frederico was talking to him, who, while we were there, looked at me a lot.

Another interesting fact happened in that ward. One of the patients mistook Nair for someone else who was his friend. He took his hand and did not let go of it. Frederico and Raimundo had to prostrate him with a pass to let go of his hand.

I went to talk to a little old man. After greetings he began to talk:

- I was a hunter, living near a small forest. I was a good shot. One day, I accidentally killed another hunter. Fearing the consequences, I put the gun in his hand as if it had gone off. It worked, and the event was given as an accident or suicide. A few years later, my daughter wanted to marry a bad boy, vagabond and cynic. Without anyone knowing, I made an appointment to go hunting with him, saying it was for a quiet conversation. I shot him and did it just like the other time. The accident was suspicious, but since there was no evidence, it all stayed there. But that spirit haunted me until I was disturbed. My family said I was lapsed. I became disembodied and suffered a lot. I have been in the hospital for a long time.

He finished talking, lowered his head and looked sad, I cheered him up; then he smiled at me.

- How good it's to have a clear conscience!

Live in the Spirit World

I went to talk to another gentleman who, soon after talking a little, told his story:

- In the incarnation before this one, I went to war, killed many men and committed many wickedness with the prisoners.

I was reincarnated in another country, poor and hard working. But some enemies found me and were waiting for an opportunity: if I made a mistake or lowered my vibration, they would obsess me. I fell in love with a wealthy girl I did not even know existed. I cheered up and confessed my love to her, but she laughed at me. I drank poison, only I did not die, I was speechless. After a while, my mother passed away. Then I was sorry and disturbed.

I wound up being a mute fool. I lived like that for years, alone in a small house, begging. Eventually, the obsessors left, I know it was my mother who made them forgive me. I was discarnates and was rescued, because I suffered resignedly for many years. I've only been here recently. I still have my "ideas" confused. Sometimes, I remember the war and I scream. But, thank God, I'm getting better, and being able to talk again is good.

He fell asleep when he got the pass.

We went to see those who were sleeping in nightmares. We formed teams of five to give passes to each of them. As we prayed, we sometimes saw their nightmares.

One lady missed her obsessor to whom she was bound by hatred and passion. She wanted him and called him non-stop. A nurse told us that the spirit that haunted her was at the Doorway, that she did not want help.

Live in the Spirit World

- Does he feel like calling you? - Laís asked the nurse.

- No, the distance is great, and the vibrations are very different. We read the nightmares of a man who had a sex drive and, to satisfy himself, killed two children.

We also saw a lady who drowned a child, a two-year-old girl, to get back at her boss

Nobody knew about it and they gave it away by accident. But one day remorse came, and she began to suffer a lot.

It was all very sad to see. Mistakes, remorse and suffering can upset someone and, when incarnated, they may have one of the mental illnesses as a reaction....

When we came to Earth for a few hours, we went to visit a sanatorium. This time, we came only to see cases of madness without obsession. Our visits help the sick: we make prayer circles and give passes. These patients almost always manifest their illnesses when they make mistakes; they feel more pain, must face responsibilities or are greeted by disagreeable events. We saw in these incarnates the diseases they had and their symptoms.

We did not have much to discuss in the final class. Only Luis asked:

- Are mental illnesses hereditary?

- Heredity can give individuals physical tendencies. However, almost always, they're reincarnated with kindred spirits and as many times as those who participate together in mistakes. They may have made mistakes together and

Live in the Spirit World

therefore redeem themselves. When the spirit is balanced, the physical brain will also be balanced.

This theme was good for all of us.

12.- OBSESSION

Live in peace with yourself is a perennial source of joy and happiness. However, when I saw for myself the work of recovery of obsessors and obsessed persons was made known to me personally, I was struck with a sadness so deep that it seemed to break my whole being, when I saw the pitiful state in which creditors and debtors, true actors representing hatred, remain, destroying each other. It's embarrassing and even painful to see the negative influence exerted by these brother's, who are still fixated on almost absolute selfishness.

The work of helping them is so difficult, it is demanding for the spirits who dedicate themselves to this mission with such great devotion and patience that we come to see in this attitude the reflection of divine love, love without borders, victorious over time and space, in the search for the recovery of His children. The Father doesn't abandon His children and helps them through His own children, involving everyone in His great love, waiting, for eternity, for us to return to the cultivation of fraternity.

Nothing better than the lessons of Allan Kardec to teach us what obsession is. It's the persistent action of a spirit upon a person. It presents different characteristics, from the simple influence of a moral order to the complete disturbance

Live in the Spirit World

of the organism and the mental faculties. The most terrible obsessions are action. Normally, the obsessor and the obsessed were related in previous existences. The obsession, subjugation and possession drive many to insanity. Usually, the obsessor tries to give the obsessed person a fixed idea. Sometimes he makes him remember part of the previous existence so that he gets confused. Almost always, between incarnated and disincarnated, or only disincarnated, where there are fights and exchanges of offenses, since hatred and passion unite them.

We came to Earth for our practical lesson, as we had seen in the hospital of the Colony, ex-obsessed, disincarnated, who were obsessed when they were incarnated. As usual, we came by airbus, stopped at an Earth Aid Station and went out to see some cases of obsession. The first we analyzed was one of simple mental influence. Such as the case of a discarnate who didn't know that he had already disincarnated and was close, "lying", on an incarnate, a girl, taking benefit of her energies, or rather, exchanging energies. She began to experience symptoms of illness, of the disincarnated's discomfort. A girl had her disembodied father, close to her.

She felt pain and sadness that began to affect her physique. We tried to intuit the mother to take her to take passes. It was a relief for us when she decided to go to a Spiritist Center. By taking the pass, the spirit also receives and feels better. The disincarnated father was invited to stay at the Spiritist Center, to be indoctrinated later, in the dispossession session.

Live in the Spirit World

Then, we saw an incarnated, religious fanatic, who had close to him a disincarnated fanatic, the two were in tune. They were always discussing religion. We watched, observed and did nothing, they both felt fine like that.

Afterwards, we went into three bars. The incarnates were drinking. And there were few who weren't accompanied by reincarnations. There, many spirits sucked the breath of those who drank, getting drunk together. Some were drunk, disincarnated, or who wanted to drink, they stayed near any incarnate who drank. Other disincarnates were there with steady company. We saw someone who was obsessed with an incarnate but did not get drunk. He wanted his obsession to drink to become ridiculous, a human rag. The discarnates drank and smoked, participating in the conversations of the incarnates. It's strange to see drunken people disincarnated. They do not differ from the incarnate ones. They fight among themselves, laugh, fall, swear. Some look like animals and for the most part they are dirty, with big hair and nails and drool. There we just watch, without being seen. We can help anyone.

- Not all the incarnated drink under the influence of the disincarnated! - commented Zé.

- Groups are aligned, both incarnated and disincarnated, and drink because they like it. Those are slaves of vices, until they're free - answered Mrs. Isaura.

- Do these disincarnated people stay like that for a long time? " asked Luíza.

- It depends on each person - answered Mrs. Isaura again. Some stay for many years, others get tired soon. They

Live in the Spirit World

are easy prey for spirits from the Doorway, who make them slaves. But when they want to leave their addiction, they always find help, either incarnated or disincarnated.

Afterwards, we went to see a group taking drugs. There were eight incarnations, only two adults, and the six young ones were already doped. I was in pain, I met some of them. We couldn't do anything either.

The group of disincarnated people taking drugs with them was larger: twenty, all disturbed. They had strange, dirty and smelly figures. The incarnated drug addicts always have those who take care of them, but the discarnate drug addicts do not; and nothing else matters to them. We surrounded them. Raimundo became visible to the disincarnated. He radiated a great light, which for a moment made them dizzy. They were afraid and tried to run away, but they could not.

Raimundo spoke to them. He invited them to a liberation, to a treatment.

After the fright, they listened in silence, but with cynical laughter. Once Raimundo finished speaking they booed. Neither of them was interested in changing. We had observed enough and left, leaving them all stoned.

Afterwards, we went to a Spiritist Center, which was a de-obsession session. There were three people obsessed with their companions.

The first case, the simplest, was a lady who was accompanied by her sister, who did not know that she had been disincarnated.

Live in the Spirit World

The fact of being disincarnated and being with family members is common, and easy to solve, because it's enough for the disincarnated person to understand his condition and be helped.

In some cases, the disincarnate come back, but generally the problem is easily solved in the Spiritist Center.

- If the obsessed person had not come to the Spiritist Center, what would happen? - Teresita asked.

- The disincarnated would eventually understand their condition, or would ask for help, or would leave. Situations like this, normally, don't last long, although they cause a lot of inconveniences - Frederico answered.

The second case was of a girl whose obsessor was in love, he was rejected in the previous existence and that's why he now obsessed her. He didn't want her to be happy or to look for a boyfriend. It was not a difficult case to solve either. Once incorporated, he received counseling and was taken to an Aid Station for treatment. The third case, which was the most difficult, would only be resolved after treatment with passes and obsession directed at both. They had been together for a long time and were so close that it was not possible to remove them without any preparation. Both were being oriented.

The Spiritist Center is undoubtedly an Aid Station for incarnated and disincarnated spirits, a support for all those who suffer. I especially love the way the Spiritist Centers are active for the good and I give thanks, for having known, when incarnated, Spiritism.

Live in the Spirit World

Finally, we went to the sanatorium. We stayed at the Aid Station, on the spiritual plane, next to the material hospital.

The Station is beautiful, simple, comfortable, very modern and equipped. The team of disincarnated there also helps the incarnated sick. We stayed there for four days. We arrived in the evening and went to rest. The next day, we went to the hall and prayed to ask Father understanding to help us with wisdom.

Many of the interns were obsessed. When they get to the point of becoming mentally ill it's because the obsession has existed for a long time; an obsession of long standing almost always damages the physical. The patients need treatment for the material. We also observed that many of the disincarnated obsessors were equally disturbed, sick as well. Many obsessions were due to revenge and collection.

We set to work. We divided into groups of three to five, to help one at a time. When these excursions arrive at hospitals and sanatoriums, the incarnates who attend to the sick always comment, "How peaceful it is around here! These days are peaceful."

Those days we helped the sick, the nurses, the doctors, in short, all those who work there. My group approached a young black girl, she was eighteen years old and next to her was a disincarnated caucasian girl. Both, in the past, in the previous incarnation, had fallen in love with the same man. The disincarnated one had committed suicide when she was rejected. In her previous incarnation, the young black woman had not been good and had made many mistakes. She

Live in the Spirit World

reincarnated with the desire to do good, and to be honest. She fell in love again with her past love. The other, disincarnated, didn't want and neither did she want to see the two together, she interfered in such a way, obsessing her rival, that she became deranged and was interned in a sanatorium. The boy married another woman, although the disincarnated one didn't know it.

The incarnated young woman talked all the time about a ball of fire, and when she talked about it, the disincarnated woman laughed out loud. The young incarnate girl talked all the time about a cook. At one time she was a cook, and when she said this, the disincarnate laughed. The fixed idea of fire was given by the disincarnate, because she committed suicide by lighting fire in her body. We tried to talk to the disincarnate, but it wasn't easy. She listened to us without understanding well, she was disturbed, and her thought was only to separate them. We made prayer circles, gave her passes and, on the fourth day, we ended up referring her to an Aid Station. She was taken to one of the infirmaries we had visited for the mentally ill in the Colony. The incarnate was also ill, but with proper treatment she would soon be well.

We saw a madam who was staying in a paid room. She belonged to an affluent family. Beside her was a black woman who obsessed her. Incarnate liked to decorate herself, and so did the obsessor friends. But it was just an appearance. When we tried to talk to the disincarnated woman, we saw that she hated the other one, but at the same time she liked to live near her. Quietly, she listened to our argument. I thought she was that hour with us. However, he said to us, cynically:

Live in the Spirit World

- Have you finished already? I have already paid too much attention to you. Please leave. The second time we spoke to her, she listened to us uneasily. When she was invited to come with us, she shouted, stamping her foot on the floor and said: "No, I'm not going!

- No is no! I am not going! Why do you want me to let her go? Why do you want her to get well? Do you know what she did to me? She was your slave, your handmaiden. She was always capricious and mean, and just because she thought I did not iron her clothes right, she threw hot water on my face and body. She also made me work all burned. The burn gets infected, I spent days between life and death. I was cured, and I was all scarred and my skin was tight, she did it to me! She did many other evils, not only to me, but also to many other slaves. Now give up, I won't go away. I'm staying with her until she discarnates.

Frederico approached and stared at her, making her see, remember why she had reacted the way she did. In the previous existence, she had been an overseer who branded slaves with a hot iron. She remembered it calmly.

- I have remembered it already! Others like you tried to take me, to teach me everything. I did it and suffered! But this one has done more and must suffer. I'm staying here!

Raimundo showed her the Colonia in all its beauty through a portable screen. She looked at it curiously, then cynical, she commented:

- This isn't for me! - Raimundo told us:

- For a long time, this woman had obsessed the other. The incarnate was in fact everything she said. In fact, she

Live in the Spirit World

reincarnated in the same family. As a teenager, her father committed suicide and it was she who found him hanged. She became disturbed and the disincarnated one was able to exercise a marked obsession. But I received an order from the Requests Department to try everything and separate them.

Raimundo approached the disembodied woman, took a good look at her, and the spots with the balls of the burn appeared on her face and arms. She began to scream:

- Wizard! This is not! It hurts so much! I do not want to remember! Take it off!

- Only if you come with us - replied Raimundo calmly.

- No!

We walked away, Raimundo told us.

- I have to take her of my own free will, it would be easy to take her by force. However, the incarnate would feel very much and might even disincarnate. If she were to come of her own free will, although I am forcing her for her own good, the incarnate will feel it, but she will not be harmed.

Raimundo watched her closely. She was writhing, crying in pain. So, attached was she to the incarnate she became restless, ran her hand over her face and arms and began to moan in pain. For eight hours, the disincarnated one endured the pain. She screamed for help. Raimundo made himself visible to her, embraced her fraternally and removed the burn.

- Daughter - said Raimundo with affection - come with us, come and be happy! You will learn many things, you will reincarnate and forget.

Live in the Spirit World

- I will - she said seriously.

- Go and say goodbye to the incarnate, take your fluids away from her.

The disincarnated woman approached the incarnate and embraced her.

- Goodbye! I'm leaving! I leave you alone. If I can, I will come back to see you.

Raimundo took her to the Colony. The incarnati's pains disappeared, but without knowing why, she began to cry. She was sad the next day, and we did everything to cheer her up. She missed the disincarnate. Frederico told us:

- She was not just obsessed. She has a lesion in her brain that got worse when she saw her father dead like that. Now, without the obsession, she will get better, but she will not heal. This is a consequence of the many mistakes she made.

We saw incarnate addicts, admitted to detox, and spirits with them, as if they were incarnate to be treated. We took as many as we could to hospitals in the Colony and in the Aid Stations.

The four days were productive, we did a lot, helped a lot, learned a lot. Back in the Colony, we were satisfied. It's good to help d. The closing class was beautiful, all the cases were commented on. Marcela sighed as she said

- How sincere forgiveness is not practiced! How wrong causes suffering! How we hurt ourselves by doing something that needs forgiveness!

Live in the Spirit World

The questions were not many, because everything we saw was well explained. But there is always something to clarify. Gloria asked:

- Frederico, can a good person be obsessed by a spirit who thinks he was harmed, but in truth he has not been?

- The disincarnate can try to approach, but if the other is good, the vibrations differ in such a way that he cannot act. Also, if the incarnate begins to get disturbed, the good ones always have help, either from other incarnates or from a disincarnate.

- And if the incarnate is not so good, but did not do anything bad to the discarnate, although he thinks he did, can he still obsess over him? - Gloria asked again.

- Obsession without major consequences is sometimes not as harmful as you think.

These people often seek help in Spiritist centers. If the person is not so good, they can be obsessed. But if the incarnate, being innocent, he will not accept it. He has his free will. What makes the spirit obsessed is that the incarnate accepts that he has a heavy conscience.

- Will the girl with the fireball heal completely? - Ilda asked.

- I think so. Often, by removing the obsessor, the physical body soon recovers or, at least, the disease is brought under control.

- We saw many disturbed obsessors. What will happen to them? - Lais asked.

Live in the Spirit World

- The day will come when they will be helped, then they will be submitted to treatments. When cured, they will either

When cured, they will study or reincarnate. But while they are wandering around, they are disturbed and troubled.

- Why could we not bring all the obsessors? - asked Cida.

- It would be good to cure everyone, to help everyone. But would that bring results? No, they would continue to make mistakes. And for the error there is no reaction? We were able to bring those that we could make want help. We argued with everyone, some wanted it, others did not. We only forced the ex-slave, because it was requested by the incarnate. Requests that came to the Department of Requests were analyzed and it was concluded that the time had come to separate them.

How nice it would be if we could take care of everyone! But since we brought many this time, there will be many more times.

Gradually they will all want the help. Only then there will be others. But suffering tires, and the obsessors suffer too.

I meditated a lot on these problems that affect many, such as obsession, and concluded:

- It's a lack of following the teachings of Jesus! He who loves his neighbor does not do evil to him. He who loves his neighbor does not persecute. He who loves to live in harmony!

13.- REQUESTS

The theory lesson was brief. Mrs. Isaura explained that we would study the petitions that the incarnated and disincarnated people make to the saints, souls or spirits, to Jesus, to Nuestra Señora, etc. There are so many petitions that in the Colonies there are departments where they're studied and sent to the teams that will attend them.

- These requests are made sometimes with faith, sometimes with the desire to make things easier for the incarnate - said Mrs. Isaura. - Some are attended to immediately, others depend on some time. For example, for help from Mary, the mother of Jesus; any good spirit nearby can help him. Those who provide these graces are spirit teams on behalf of some entity. It does not matter. Honors to the incarnate are important only to themselves. We, disincarnated workers of good, care only about the good we do.

- Is it wrong to make promises? - Gloria asked.

- Many do it in good faith, but it is time to understand that you cannot exchange material goods for spiritual favors. It's very petty: you do this, I will do that. You can ask, but knowing that if you respond, you do not have to give anything in return. It's enough to say thank you.

Live in the Spirit World

- What is there to ask for? - Ivo asked.

- The right thing to do is to do it yourself. But you can ask to improve, to have patience, strength, wisdom, to change vices for virtues. This is more possible.

- Many people make promises - Joaquim said. - My mother made one for me to keep, but I disincarnated and didn't keep it. That was why she thought I was in hell. She suffered and passed on her agony to me. The priest advised her to do it herself. My mother complied and gave me peace of mind. I suffered a lot when she imagined me in hell.

- The non-fulfillment of what one has promised brothers. I know people who disincarnate and have no peace, they wander with anguish for not having fulfilled a promise. Others did not fulfill and even forgot; after being rescued, they learn that this fact doesn't interfere in helping them when they disincarnate. Good spirits don't charge. It's our custom to charge ourselves. But as we promise, exchange favors, and receive help from others, it's honest to keep our promise. You cannot promise something for another to fulfill. We are not responsible for the requests and promises of others. When earthlings evolve, there will be no promises.

- Are there those who make promises whose fulfillment is their inner improvement? - Lauro asked.

- Very few. They promise a lot and sometimes things that are very difficult to fulfill! They rarely promise to improve themselves, to give up an addiction.

During the practical class we got to know the Request Department. They are not the same, they vary a lot from one Colony to another. In the larger Colonies, or those close to

Live in the Spirit World

where, on the physical plane, there are pilgrimages, these Departments are big. In the Colony Saint Stephan it's located inside the Religions building. It has four great halls. The first one deals with the petitions of the disincarnated spirits. Without the physical clothing, we ask for much less. There aren't promises made, but we are educated in gratitude. There, in this hall, there come petitions from disincarnated spirits in the Colony and in the Aid Stations. They're requests for change of work, change of housing and, many of them, to help their dear loved ones, disincarnated or incarnated.

The other three rooms are used to deal with requests from incarnates. In the first one, they are separated and to the other two rooms for analysis, and then they return to their room of origin to be sent to the rescuers or to the spirits working in this Department, that is, those that can be attended to.

There are not many requests without promises, that's why the second hall is small. Many of them are taken attention of. This room is very nice and has beautiful paintings on the wall.

The whole department is painted light yellow and decorated with many flower pots. The third hall, is bigger and with several tables, is for those who make petitions with promises. The petitions are separated there, and the tables have cards with names of Saints, of Jesus, of Souls. Those sent to the Virgin Mary are numerous. They then separate the viable ones from the unfeasible ones. Those considered unfeasible will not be attended to, as in the cases of petitions for rain or not rain, for the victory of sports teams, for winning the lottery, etc. Viable requests are those that can be

Live in the Spirit World

fulfilled, in part or in full. In this case, the petitioners are visited by workers of the Department, who give their final opinion. If it's approved, the workers attend to it and the person obtains the grace, so it remains for the petitioner to fulfill the promise.

All this is recorded in well-organized files. These include the name of the person asking, the address and what is being asked for. Once the request has been made, the people of the Department take note of it. For example: if the person asks in a church, a worker registers it and takes the request to the appropriate place. But some requests come directly to the Department. The thought acts as a telephone, as if the petitioner with faith communicates in this way.

This isn't the case with all people, but it's enough to have faith for it to happen. Doubting cuts off the connection.

- That's why many people ask people they consider good, people who have faith, to pray for them", said Zé.

Most of the requests come from places like churches, cemeteries, homes, etc. Those are written down and taken to the Department. And this isn't only done by those who work there, but also by any kindred spirits, and sometimes they are family spirits or workers from any other sector. In the cemeteries, the rescuers there take notes.

We were curious and observing everything, when a supervisor of the house told us kindly:

- You can read the petitions, but please put it, afterwards, in the same place.

Live in the Spirit World

I was surprised by the quantity. I took a few that seemed viable. Among the requests were those to stop smoking, another one to accept the son I hadn't been able to love. There were also suggestions for rescuers.

The file of the mother, who asked the Virgin for help in loving her son, and it was seen that mother and son had been enemies in the past and that, in this incarnation, they were together to be reconciled. Help consisted of talking to her while her body slept and making her understand the need to accept her son. Involving her in daily thoughts for six months, encouraging her to forgive and love.

- Will it work? - I asked a worker, showing him the file.

- I think it will. It will depend on whether she accepts our guidelines, he replied kindly.

A lot is asked of us, and a stack of unfeasible requests was large. I took a few to read. In one a madam asked for help from the souls in purgatory so that her husband would not discover that she had betrayed him; she would pray three prayer beads in the cemetery.

Another time, a young man asked St. Antonio to help him marry a good-looking rich girl, who would go to mass once a month for the rest of his life.

And a certain girl prayed to the Virgin Mary to save her from becoming pregnant; she was single. Some, unfeasible, insisted with petitions to several saints at the same time and with unbelievable promises.

The Department's counselor was kind enough to enlighten us:

Live in the Spirit World

- We respect all forms of belief and all requests". If they have made it this far, it's because they were made in faith, although we know that many are not based on reasoned faith. We respect even the requests to cover up mistakes, like this one who asks for protection to the Virgin of Aparecida so as not to be arrested while stealing. There's more ignorance than evil in that one.

Marcela read aloud the words of a drug trafficker who asked for protection so as not to be discovered or arrested. He had promised to provide a huge sum of money in alms to the poor. The counselor explained:

- Every time this petitioner is about to receive a shipment of toxic substances, he goes like this.

We don't help him, we cannot help him as he wishes, and events are left to chance. For some time, he has been promising, and as he hasn't been stopped, he pays his promise. We've already tried to help him, encouraging him to change his way of life, to stop trafficking. But, unfortunately, that isn't what he wants, because he likes what he does.

After analyzing everything, we went with a group of rescuers who were going to attend to some requests.

The first case was that of a man who was asking to be cured. He was in a hospital and had advanced stage cancer.

He would not be treated in his body, his request wouldn't be granted, but he would be helped in another way. The helpers would assist him and encourage him to think good thoughts and resign himself. The team would visit him every day, until he became disincarnated. He felt our

Live in the Spirit World

presence and received the donated fluids, calmed down and went to sleep.

Another request moved us. An eight-year-old girl, motherless, wished for her mother to return.

- But is that not impractical? - asked Gloria.

- The order, yes - answered Federico -, but not the help. Besides, for a certain period, the helpers will visit her every day, console her and help her to accept her mother's reincarnation.

Another madam wanted help because she was feeling sick, she was short of breath. A discarnate was at her side, taking advantage of her. The first responders made themselves visible to her, talked to him and convinced him to go to an Aid Station.

Then we went to see how the records are written. It was at a church. That afternoon, it was almost empty. There was only one good worker there. We went up to a lady who was praying with faith at the foot of the altar of the Heart of Jesus. The good worker took her request as she prayed. She wanted her son to pass school.

- Will this woman be attended to? - Ivo asked the worker.

- Department workers can go to their children and encourage them to study. Sometimes, he may have a health problem or some discarnate person disturbing him. The mother is then advised, in the form of intuition, to seek a doctor or a Spiritist Center. Knowing the cause, the workers

Live in the Spirit World

can find a solution. But if it's laziness, it can only be encouraged. No one will do what they should: study.

Afterwards, we went to a place of pilgrimage. There many people were paying promises or asking for graces. The requests were diverse: they hoped to obtain facilities, wealth. Some were touching: they asked for health, to improve their character.

The latter, in fact, were usually done for other people, such as the wife who wanted the partner to stop drinking and the son, to stop taking drugs.

In the places of pilgrimage there are large teams of workers. Requests are usually sent to a department of the Colony. If the place is very popular, the Department is there, as in *Aparecida do Norte*. There, a large team works there, where requests are written down and then taken to the rooms built on the Astral Plane, as a continued construction of the material.

- Are the places of pilgrimage attacked by the brothers of the Doorway? - Cida asked.

- Yes, that's why the workers are also guards, and the place is equipped with electric lightning - answered Raimundo.

- What happens if lightning strikes an incarnate? - Joaquim asked.

- Nothing, it only reaches the disincarnated - Raimundo continued to explain. - The workers are trained to deal with these lightning strikes, and there are no mishaps.

Live in the Spirit World

Because many people come from far away, from different parts of Brazil, the rescuers then go to their homes. All requests are answered.

We saw one man ask to win a car in the raffle. The workers weren't going to interfere in the raffle.

But they were going to encourage him to think more spiritually.

In times of large pilgrimages, the place gets extra helpers. It's touching to be there listening to the petitions - there are so many people of faith! We didn't work during the study we did, we just observed.

We returned to the Colony. The final class, as always, served to clear up any doubts. Joaquim was the first to ask:

- How is the help to requests that require time, like that of a gentleman who asked for protection to his grandson who was just born?

Frederico answered:

- That is not feasible. The newborn won't have special protection because of the request Help, at any moment, we all have it. But the request of another woman who prays all her life for a good death or disincarnation, then there it's, when the time comes, she will have help. If it's good, she will have a more profound help, if not, only assistance to disengage it and give her the first guidelines.

- A madam asked the Virgin Mary with faith to help her disincarnated husband. How is the help done? - Rosalia asked.

Live in the Spirit World

- The helpers can search and find out where the husband is. If he is well, nothing will be done. If you are suffering, the case is analyzed. He may not want help at this time, so he will not get help and the request can't be granted. But if he is suffering and wants help, you will get help.

- We saw a woman who made too many promises, for nothing. What will happen to her - Ivo asked.

- She is doing the wrong thing; they have already tried to instruct her, to guide her to change. Requests of everyday events take their course. The workers cannot waste time on this. We want her to change, but if she doesn't, nothing will happen to her. We have seen that she isn't acting in bad faith.

- A lot is asked whether it rains or not - Ilda said - Are they all unfeasible?

- Yes, everyone.

- I was impressed by a madam who prayed to die, to disincarnate - said Lauro.

- The request is not viable, but she will receive help. They will encourage her to want to live in the incarnation, they will try to get someone, in the incarnation, to talk to her and help her. She won't disincarnate out of time. No one can be helped to disincarnate like this.

- In case of danger, does the command go through the Department? - Cida asked.

Live in the Spirit World

- No, good spirits are always trying to help in any way possible.

- What if there is no one around? - Cida asked again.

- The words stay in the air and can be picked up by good spirits within a radius of kilometers. It can go to the Department in a matter of seconds and the personnel there will notify a team working on Earth.

When you return quickly, help arrives immediately.

- Only requests made in faith go to the Department, don't they? - Teresita asked.

- Yes. You can't imagine how much they ask for. But those made without faith do not reach the Department.

- If someone makes a promise and the request isn't for the Department, but it turns out to be successful; does the person have to keep the promise? - James asked.

- Whoever made the promise will not know this detail. The uncompiled promise bothers one's self. The promises of the requests to which the people of the Department attend, in the name of Jesus, Mary, the saints, etc., it does not matter if these are complied with or not. For the workers it is enough to do good, to do a good job.

- Are there spirits that demand promises? - Marcela asked.

Live in the Spirit World

- There are promises made in religious houses to some spirits, to the souls in "Purgatory". Those who attend are spirits not yet enlightened. They help as best they can, but they want to be paid and they usually charge.

The questions ended and Frederico finished with these words:

- When the Earth evolves, this exchange of favors will cease. The requests will be a help to improve. However, we have already learned that everyone must do for himself what is due to him.

14.- THE DOORWAY

We had a few hours to spare before starting the new theme of study: The Doorway. I took the opportunity to meditate, and memories came to my mind... I remembered what my father once told us in the warmth of our home, about the Doorway. Nature does not deviate from the path of improvement, of divine manifestation. Wherever we look, there is evolution, even slow, but constant. It seems to us that only in human life there is the possibility of refusing this growth, although many do not admit it. But if there is not evolution, there is stagnation on the egoistic mental plane. It's a clear truth, so aggressively exposed in the regions of the Doorway, that it makes us tremble.

It seems to be the home of all imaginable miseries. Spirits who turn into human rags, cultivating promiscuity, fear, misery and exploitation among themselves by the most shrewd and violent.

Nature always seems to be frowning and displeased, because the day never fully dawns, and the darkness is constant. Sometimes violent storms lash these regions, in a supreme effort to relieve, cleanse the accumulations of impurities or stains and darkness created by a deeply selfish man.

Live in the Spirit World

There they gather, in depressing coexistence, negligent spirits who, on Earth, were not concerned with spiritual growth, because if they did not do evil, they didn't do good either, and thus created debts. Because, when you can grow spiritually, you must do it, so we can reflect the light, the harmony, the goodness and the brotherhood of God.

The Doorway is not certainly a pleasant place. If most incarnates had an idea of what it's like to be living in it, even if it's only for a certain time, they would make more use the incarnation period more to learn, live in goodness and change internally, making themselves worthy of better to have a better home when they discarnate.

I never thought I would see so many different things as there were at the Doorway conference. The films were separated by elements. First, we saw films about vegetation. At the Doorway, it's always small and not made up of many species. For the most part, the trees are twisted, with thick trunks and not too tall. In some places, there is undergrowth reminiscent of the herbs and grasses of the Earth. They serve as food for many spirits that live there. The vegetation varies according to the different regions of the Doorway. We have seen first that of our region, then that of Brazil and, finally, that of the world.

Then they showed some species of animals, such as birds, which are also of a few species, devoid of beauty, but useful.

We saw the various forms of caverns, caves and abysses in the Doorway.

Live in the Spirit World

- All this exists because there are those who lived in it - said Mrs. Isaura.

Films showed the different types of inhabitants of the Doorway, who can be divided into groups. The bosses, intelligent spirits, usually scholars of magic, eager to dominate, almost always hate the good and the good guys. They are mostly sorcerers. The big bosses usually have a common human appearance. With extravagant forms, only underbosses and underlings present themselves.

There are those who work with the bosses, the members of the group, the gang. There are also scholars, sorcerers, and experts in natural laws. They obey the rules of the group. Although they consider themselves free, they are not, because they don't easily leave the group and receive punishments for disobedience. They say they like who they are and the way they are and live.

Solitary spirits are also found at the Doorway, but they are few. Most of them do live in groups. There are those who wander, in rowdy groups, between the Doorway and Earth.

There are slaves, those who do not belong to the gang, they work, they receive nothing in return, except punishment if they do not obey.

There are also those who are tortured and treated like this, mostly out of revenge.

Just as there are those who say they like it, there are also those who consider the Doorway a hell, they suffer from wandering aimlessly, suffering for their mistakes.

Live in the Spirit World

They cluster in cities, small towns or nuclei. We have seen many cities in the movies, all of them have the same base. The best building is for the boss, it's the place for parties and the courtroom or hearings, most of them have a library with books on magic and obscene themes. Most of the books and magazines are also published on Earth.

But the incarnates have books and magazines that are good and bad, while only bad ones are there. We saw, astonished, large cities with many enslaved inhabitants.

The American Doorway is milder than in Europe and Asia. The Doorway of the old world is more closed, with huge and horrible abysses.

We watched many movies about each Doorway in other regions, because in the practical class we would only visit the one in our region.

- Why are these bosses allowed to exist? - Rosalia asked, impressed by the power they have.

- We all have our free will - answered Raimundo. They are what we want to be. They are allowed everything, but not everything suits us. They are spirits eager for the allure of power.

- Wouldn't it be interesting for a team of good spirits to indoctrinate them? - Rosalia asked again.

- There would be others. Many waits for a vacancy for a chief. Among them there's always the dispute for leadership. Only when they show signs of weariness is there an opportunity for change. But they, being smart, know that someday they will have to change.

Live in the Spirit World

- They aren't afraid of being expelled from Earth when it changes from a planet of atonement to one of regeneration? - asked Ivo -. Or don't they know?

- They know, but they always think that there is time, that this fact will take time. Others don't care, because the power goes to their heads. We know that we, a large part of the people, were expelled from another planet, which went from a world of testing to a world of regeneration, and here we begin to learn again. On Earth, too, there will be a selection and only the good and those who intend to be good with good will and sincerity will remain.

The Doorway is not pleasant to see in the movies. Knowing that this is reality and that our brothers are there saddened me for a moment.

Then I meditated on what Mrs. Isaura said:

- Doorway is not synonymous with suffering or happiness, it's a transitory place. It's an environment created by the misuse of the human mind. Not everyone finds the Doorway sad and ugly, many like to live there. Tastes differ, some like cleanliness, others like dirt. Some prefer truth, others prefer illusion and lies. After all, no one is there because of punishment, but to vibrate like the environment. Those who suffer are not there forever, there is help.

The theory class was great, we saw a lot about the Doorway, and there is a lot to see and study. We didn't go deep, because our study time was just to know the main thing. The Doorway is immense, the size of continents. Wherever there's a nucleus of incarnates, there will also be a good and a bad spiritual space.

Live in the Spirit World

The nuclei are groupings of spirits. I have been surprised by some nuclei, such as the suicidal ones, which are almost always in the valleys and are frequented by both rescuers and bad ones, who go on to torment those who live there even more.

Drug addicts' centers are almost always in small towns. In some places they're in large, closed and busy cities, where they have big parties. The place where the drug addicts of the region are is called the Valley of the Dolls. There are houses and a big laboratory there. We've seen, in movies, how it's inside, including the laboratory.

Other similar groups tune in and form nuclei of thieves, murderers, etc.

We studied our region's Doorway again. We looked at the map and everything there is marked and divided into numbered parts by sector, so that rescuers have their work easier.

In our region, there's a medium-sized Doorway city with many cores. Most of them are named by their inhabitants. Some are interesting, others ridiculous or obscene. There is a nucleus of alcoholics called Big Barrel. It has a few houses spliced together. The boss and other slaves live there, but they aren't tortured ones. Its inhabitants also like to wander among the incarnated and get drunk with them.

I was not very enthusiastic about the practical class. I knew I had to get to know the Doorway, and, for me, it was not encouraging. But it exists and can't be ignored.

Live in the Spirit World

We left early in the morning, by airbus, to the Charity and Light Shelter. There we stayed for a few days, touring during the day and resting at night. But we also hiked for two nights at the Doorway. The first day, we went around the Station. On these excursions, we would help those who sincerely asked us for help.

The ground there is diversified, sometimes muddy, sometimes slippery or dry. We put on the special clothes I have already mentioned and put on thick gloves. Here, many spirits go to the Doorway without anything, dressing normally, but for us, because it was a study, these clothes were recommended. Blue Flower on these excursions was close to me, but our friend worked hard, always cheerful and happy.

Seeing the Doorway in person is different from hearing about it, talking about it, reading a story or watching a movie. It also differs according to the taste of the narrator. While I know its existence is useful and necessary, I found it an ugly and horrible place. I've been thanked, many times, for not wandering, in my disembodiment, through these places and for knowing it only in the studio.

The Doorway follows the rhythm of the Earth, whether it's day or night in the region of the incarnation, whether it rains or not, whether it is cold or hot, it's the same there.

In the Doorway, the smell is unpleasant, it smells of earth, rotten mud and mildew. The air is heavy and suffocating.

Live in the Spirit World

In its most pleasant part is the region where the Charity and Light Shelter is located, there the vegetation is greater, and scarcer in the most recondite zones. In the caves, there is not any vegetation and if there is, it's very little.

Each of us carried a backpack containing a flashlight, a small safety net, a small safety rod, sheets to wrap the rescued, because these unfortunate ones are usually in tattered clothes or sometimes naked.

This time we could talk. When we heard voices, cries for help, we went to them. We approached, talked to the needy, explaining what our assistance consisted of. That they would be taken to the Station, where through discipline and order, they would be healed, but they would have to be willing to change their lives. Some wanted to be free from there, sometimes they were in caves, holes or in the mud. They wanted social assistance, but they weren't willing to change or go to the shelter. Those who did not want to come with us, we simply pulled them out of the holes, caves or mud, cleaned them up and let them go wherever they wanted. Most of them wandered.

During the excursion, we met many of them. Some asked us to take them to where the incarnates were, and we told them we couldn't. In fact, we weren't ordered to take them or teach them to do that.

- If they go to the incarnates, they will torment and vampirize them - said Joaquim. But, unfortunately, the residents here teach many to do that.

- Do they not know how to go on their own? - Ivo asked Joaquim.

Live in the Spirit World

- It's very difficult to go without knowing the way.

We saw some guards from the city of the Doorway watching over spirits trapped in holes, mud, etc. They do not like to be released, but they almost always go with the good guys. We were in a large group. Besides us, there were thirty other members, so we were accompanied by three instructors, Blue Flower and five other Station workers. Some groups attacked us, throwing dirt, stinking mud, stones, etc. at us. We opened our nets and tried to talk to them. If they didn't stop the attack, we would respond with our lightning rods and they would run away.

- If a big group attacks us? - Nair asked with concern.

- The bigger gangs will not be interested in confronting us - said Raimundo. But, if we feel the presence of a major attack, we'll return to the outpost immediately.

We have studied the vegetation, we have approached, we have passed the hand, we went to the water filters, we studied the ground, the stones. We were distracted while looking at the stones, when Raimundo asked us to gather.

- In a few minutes, we're going to be attacked. Soon we heard blasphemies, screams and howls.

- And the cheating teacher who's teaching the class and his ugly students - said a voice, shouting.

- We do not want conversations. You can defend yourselves because we are going to attack. you cheeky! We are not going to where you are living to study anything. You have nothing to do here. You want to copy the landscape? You must pay!

Live in the Spirit World

They laughed outrageously. We opened the nets and fell silent. We stayed, Nair and I, near Blue Flower. Rosalia was afraid and Frederico had to protect her. They threw various filth at us.

- Are they not going to stop? - asked Raimundo in a loud voice -. We are here in peace! Laughter and screams were the answer, and they continued attacking us.

- To the rays! - said Raimundo

Some of us shoot with lightning rods. The projectiles cleared the place. They resisted for minutes, hiding behind the rocks. But many will be hit, down, paralyzed for hours. Those who are hit have the feeling that they are dying again. Little by little they will retreat, they stopped laughing, but they still blasphemed.

When they all left, we put away our nets.

- I confess I was afraid - said Zé -. If I were a woman, I would be leaning against one of the instructors as they did.

Rosalia, Nair and Patricia. Raimundo, do they not have a firearm? I see them with rudimentary weapons.

- They are the ones who know how to do it. The intelligent spirits here at the Doorway use their minds to attack. Then, with a firearm, the bullets go through the bodies, only wounding them. They prefer sticks, chains, which is what they use, and they are more afraid of them.

- They have no nets or lightning bolts - observed Luis. If so, could we defend ourselves against them?

- If one of us loses the lightning rod or the net, will they know how to use them?

Live in the Spirit World

- If one of us loses them, it's carelessness. We must be careful with our objects. But if that happens, both the net and the lightning rods will self-destruct if used by someone with low vibration.

- Do they not know how to build them? - Luíza asked

- They do not know. But if they build similar weapons, use them with each other, nothing would happen to us if we were attacked. As a precaution, we wear these clothes and bring our equipment. You're a student, you don't have the knowledge yet to come here without these materials.

The storm we wanted to see happened. It got darker. We huddled close to each other and watched. The strong wind whistled, shaking the trees. We understand why they are low and strong.

Lightning cut through the air, brightening everything, the thunder was violent, the noise deafening. Soon the rain began to fall, leaving even more mud on the ground. It did not last more than thirty minutes. Then the air became lighter, less suffocating, and the smell was milder.

For days we walked, entered caves, descended into holes. The caverns or caves there are not large, but we saw some huge ones in the movies. These places were not beautiful like many on Earth. They are all very similar.

The stones are dark and without beauty, it's cold inside, there is a corridor where spirits are usually trapped. It's quite easy to get lost. The darkness is total.

The nights at the shelter were pleasant, we talked, listened to music, exchanged ideas of what we saw, ate and

Live in the Spirit World

rested in our rooms or lodging. The instructors and Blue Flower did not stay with us, they went to the rooms to work. Every day we brought in rescues that needed attention.

We went out for two nights but stayed close to the Shelter. The night at Doorway is more terrifying. You only see the moon, when it's full, being reddish. The night is very dark there.

After getting to know all the Doorway around the Shelter, we set out on foot in the morning to the Observation Station.

15.- GETTING TO KNOW THE DOORWAY BETTER

We did not need to go quietly to the Observation Station, but we only spoke when necessary; we did not feel like talking, as we were concentrating on watching everything.

The way is not easy, we were walking next to each other, paying attention to where we were stepping. In the theory class, we studied the path on the map and we had already passed that way when we visited the Observation Station. But we needed experience so that we would not get lost on that curvy path. The further we walked, the darker it got. We were helping the brothers we met. They were the ones who fell in the mud, the ones who crawled on the ground. We sympathized with everyone. Some, even suffering, when they saw us, shouted insults at us:

- What are you doing here? You should not be hanging around here watching. Go away!

Many spoke obscene words. Groups of troublemakers almost always run away from rescue teams.

We've encountered such groups twice, fleeing scandalously making a ruckus. The smarter ones just stop

Live in the Spirit World

and watch, they do not swear, they keep quiet. The bullies, who like fights, confront the rescue groups, but at the first impact of lightning, they run away shouting and insulting.

On the way, we welcomed twenty-three sick people and took them to the Station. Some were sheltered, others on stretchers.

When we arrived at the Station, five of those twenty-three said they did not want to stay. But before we let them go, we cleaned and dressed them; the wounded, we bandaged them, fed them and then let them go. The remaining eighteen were cleaned and sent to the wards.

An interesting fact: one of those who did not stay, despite being clean and fed, we found him days later, recognizing him by his clothes, he was with a group that insulted us.

We always arrived at the Station tired and after cleaning up and eating, we listened to music and talked.

We did not work at the Station, only the instructors did.

One day we saw a big storm, when we were at the Doorway, near the Vigil. It was frightening. Lightning shot through the place with huge flashes. Groups ran from one place to another, scared, not knowing where to go. Many approached us, but when the storm calmed down, they escaped.

- Is there no danger of a lightning strike? - Lauro asked Frederico.

Live in the Spirit World

- No. The lightning does not do any harm. They burn harmful fluids. Our sheaths protect us from them. But, if it falls on one of the wanderers, they will receive an electric charge that will make him lose his senses, since he cannot disembody again[2].

The desire that one gives when one walks the Doorway is to help everyone; however, the green fruits are not taken advantage of. Not everyone wants the help of the good ones. It's not possible to take those who do not want to, since they would be detrimental to the Stations and Colonies. When you sincerely aspire to ask for help, you will always have someone to help you.

We climbed into a hole. We put our flashlights on our foreheads and descended with ropes, which we tied to a device that we fixed to the ground. We all climbed down, only Raimundo stayed there. After a few minutes, we found a large slope of about ten meters. There were spirits that rushed to meet us asking for help. We organized them to climb up. There were eight of them. Five managed to climb up by themselves, one needed one of the Station workers to put him on his back. Two were unconscious, and had to go on a stretcher, which we tied to the ropes and lifted. Up there, Raimundo spoke to them and explained how the help would be and that, if they wanted to, they could leave. Only the unconscious was taken without asking. Many stayed with us, but the majority almost always left without thanks.

---

[2] Spiritual Author's Note: Storms occur at the Doorway as they do on Earth. If we can predict them here, so can we at the Aid Stations. They are not sent by the Major Plane, but may be, at times, out of necessity. Storms are part of everyday life on the Doorway.

Live in the Spirit World

We continued down and stopped at a cave. The darkness was total darkness. We went in, it was not large, there were six spirits there, three of whom asked to stay. That was strange. They all asked:

- Why?

Mrs. Isaura simply answered:

- They like it. Everyone must have their own reason for not wanting to leave here.

We continued descending, we reached the end. It was a ditch and there were three spirits tied with ropes; we let them go.

- Who arrested them, why? - James wanted to know.

Two of them cursed their tormentors and asked us in the name of God to punish them. The third was silent.

Mrs. Isaura answered:

- That's why they are here, to curse. And certainly, for fighting. We can release them, take them to the top, but not to the Station. Returning to what was quiet, Mrs. Isaura asked:

- And you, do not you want revenge?

- No, madam, I want to go with you. I suffer, and I am tired.

- You coward! - said one of the two.

- You will go with us - said our instructor.

We saw other things like on the tour. When they were rescued, they asked us to avenge them, to arrest their executioners right there.

Live in the Spirit World

We went back up, the hole was deep, I thought it was horrible and I knew it was one of the little ones.

That night, Blue Flower stayed with us for a while. He said that in China the Doorway is more terrifying and that there are places so closed that rescuers rarely go there.

A rescuer from the Station explained to us:

- Those we released from the hole who did not come with us will soon be involved in new fights and, many times, will be arrested again. It's only on study trips that they are released; like the ones we do every day. We only go to those who ask for help.

The next day, we entered a large cave. We tied ropes around our waists, so we wouldn't get lost.

We did not go into the lowest places. We pulled out many spirits but helped few.

We went to see some cores up close. They are all the same: small villages, with few houses grouped together. Some cores are enclosed by high walls. We did not go into any of them. That day, Artur came to keep us company. Artur is my father's disincarnated co-worker. I like him a lot.

Cheerful and laughing, he greeted us smiling and said he would join us on the excursion at the Doorway.

We were delighted.

We heard a large band approaching in a place filled with stones. We gathered in a circle. Blue Flower was next to me and each instructor was also close by. A large group of about three hundred residents of the Doorway stopped in front of us. They quietened and one of them said:

Live in the Spirit World

- Is that where the daughter of the sorcerer José Carlos is?

I had already heard spirits refer to my father with contempt, calling him a sorcerer.

Artur took a few steps forward and stopped in front of them, folded his arms across his chest and replied:

- Yes, why?

From his mind came flashes of light that hit them hard. For seconds they received the rays of light, then, frightened, they burst into screams. Artur returned to our quiet group:

- Should we continue?

We were all curious and surrounded him asking:

- What happened? - Many asked at the same time.

- We knew they were going to attack you and I came to help you - Artur said, as calm as ever.

- Did you want Patricia? - asked Nair, surprised.

- They only wanted to scare her.

- Why was that? - asked Ivo.

- Patricia's father is a spiritist counselor and disturbs the idle, who for a while prefer the path of error. They thought they could frighten their daughter, but they forgot that the incarnate ones who work for good have the good disincarnate ones to help them.

- Will they come back? - Luíza asked.

- I don't think so. But I will continue with you until the end of the study of the Doorway.

Live in the Spirit World

- Were you afraid, Patricia? - asked Zé.

- No, I felt as calm as always - I said, looking at Blue Flower.

How can we not be trusted if we have the company of the three instructors, Blue Flower and Artur? In fact, Artur offered us his company in the excursions we made to the Doorway, he was not staying at the Station. He was always silent and answered when asked, being kind to everyone. Artur is simple, no one guesses what he is capable of.

For that we admire him and are grateful to him.

The Samaritans went out with us. They know the Doorway better than its residents. It's good to go out with them. They took us to swamp number two, so called because it's a muddy area. It's difficult to access the place, you must go down a lot and there are many chasms. We went down and helped brothers in need, but only a few would go to the Station, most of them would just be taken out of there. The place is ugly, there is a lot of mud, little vegetation, and it's dark and smelly. It was too late to return, it would soon be night, it was then that Frederico, Mrs. Isaura and Raimundo joined in their thoughts and made a path of light. It's beautiful! Wonderful! It's a sloping road of yellowish light.

We were walking on it. It was strange and phenomenal. It's like walking on the ground. After walking for hours on rough ground, it was pleasant to walk on the light walkway. The three instructors stepped forward and formed a walkway two meters in front of them. We went behind with the rescued and, as we passed, the walkway was disappearing.

Live in the Spirit World

We had to help hold it with good thoughts. We went singing. Soon we were on dry land and close to the Observation Station. From a distance, the gangway, although light yellow, looked like a rainbow.

The next day, Raimundo asked the head of the Doorway for permission to go in and see her. The Governor, as he is called, gave permission, but warned us that we would be observed.

Obviously, we could only visit some areas, so we could not see the prisons, the places of torture and we didn't even enter the houses of the residents. We visited the party hall, everything was red and yellow-hot, with drawings in black. On the walls there are drawings of dragons, satanic figures, like how the incarnates draw the devil.

Also adorning the place were yellow and red curtains in a strong tone. There are no flowers or plants. There were some chairs in the place. Then we went to the courtroom, which was scary. Everything was black, with gold and silver trim. There were many chairs, all black and in order. The place was not dirty at all. We also went to the library, it's big, containing many magazines and books about sex, many were copies that the incarnated have. They were not messy. They are on the shelves and there are even those who take care of the books and magazines.

I stayed close to Artur the whole time, but he did not talk much. We were visitors and were advised to avoid comments. We walked through the streets, which were reasonably clean on this occasion. The streets are curved and made of stones.

Live in the Spirit World

When it was time to leave, Raimundo thanked them for the welcome. There was no response, as they think they are important. When we left, two guards came to look at us, to see if we were taking anyone from the city. We did not help anyone, nor did we see anyone to help. We could see only the residents, who did their best to show us how happy they were. But they aren't, because their joy is fake. No one is that happy, in the right term, far from the Father, from God.

Raimundo explained that these visits are not always allowed and that, without authorization, no excursion enters the city. The slaves and tortured people are hidden in opportunities like these. However, when the rescuers see fit, they go unnoticed and help those who ask for help.

We thank the Samaritans, Artur and the Observation Station staff. We said goodbye happily, the excursion was over. We went to the Shelter and from there to the Colony.

At the Colony, we received eight hours free of charge. I went to see grandma and friends, it's so good to see them again!

After that, we had the concluding class. There was not much to ask. Only James asked Raimundo:

- Why do so many of the sufferers stay in the valleys and holes and not in their cities?

- Because, in the cities, they don't want the suffering, the disturbed or the unconscious, because they are useless.

We were all dismayed to see the Doorway. But now we knew how to cross it and go to the rescue.

Live in the Spirit World

At the end of the class, we said a prayer for those who do live there and gave thanks for not being in it.

Happy are those who make every effort to vibrate in good. Blessed are those who, when disincarnated, are worthy of a place of bliss. Happy are those who follow the teachings of Jesus; those who learn, incarnated, what it's to disincarnate and change internally to be better. These won't have the Doorway as their dwelling place.

16.- DEVICES AND MINDS

We had a theoretical lesson on devices used in the spiritual realm. Unfortunately, I cannot describe them in detail for two reasons. First, I do not have the means to be able to transmit them, and the medium, not knowing them, finds it difficult.

Secondly, the Higher Plan did not authorize me to describe them in detail, because this narrative, being public, can also be read by the bad guys.

On the spiritual plane there are many devices. They are all beautiful and useful. We already knew them all, many of them we use for excursions and daily life in the Colony. None of them pollute or cause accidents. Accidents do not happen here.

I will start by telling you about the wonderful airbus, a mobility vehicle, a mixture of buses and airplanes used to travel short and long distances, for small groups or many people.

The screens, used in many Spiritist Centers by disincarnated workers so that people can see events, especially of the past, are light, simple and very practical.

There is the air remover, a device used to collect fluids, either the good ones, which are stored; or the bad ones, to

Live in the Spirit World

clean the environment. It resembles a small vacuum cleaner of those on Earth, it's light and practical.

There are devices used mainly in the Aid Stations, to maintain the environment with a pleasant temperature. They are installed in one part of the building.

There are devices to keep an eye on things and those that measure vibrations. There are also defense devices and lightning launchers, which look like a ball launcher. They are light, and there are those that are small, eight centimeters.

There are also devices like television and videos. There are many, all useful and wonderful.

The spirits of the Doorway also have many devices that they use. In class, we learn how to use and neutralize them.

In class, we had knowledge of all the devices that exist on the spirit plane. We learned how to use them, but not how to build them. There are workshops in the Colonies for such procedures.

We only had the theoretical part, in which we handled various devices. Neither did we have the concluding class, because the doubts were solved during the theoretical class.

We talked a lot, exchanging ideas. I told my colleagues a fact of my knowledge.

- The Spiritist Center I was attending, when I was incarnated, received, during a certain period, the help of a group of spirits coming from a place called Colina. They are all oriental, Blue Flower is part of this group. These spirits are all enchanting, just like Blue Flower. Among them, there is a

Live in the Spirit World

special doctor named Tachá. He's an excellent device builder, but the most impressive thing is his way of healing his patients. With joy, grace, contagious kindness, he wraps his patients in a soft and harmonious song, while recovering their spirit. The result is astonishing. After disembodiment, I asked Mauricio, a medical friend who also worked with this team, why Tachá has such ease and speed in healing. He told me that, while he, Mauricio, healed the patient from the outside in, Tachá enveloped the patient with music, making him initiate his own internal change, helping himself. While we, Mauricio said, with our way of doing everything alone, he makes the patient recover by himself; hence his ability.

- These devices were described in the book Violets on the Window.

Then we had a lesson on the influence of the mind. We know well that we can influence and that we can be influenced for both good and evil. Evil minds can harm others: disincarnated to other disincarnated, disincarnated to incarnates, and incarnates to other incarnates.

- You should, they should influence, try to transmit to others good thoughts, of joy, peace and love - said Frederico.

The mind has a lot of strength. Trained minds do a lot. We saw in movies several ways to use the mind, either for good or for bad.

You can create and shape objects with your mind. We tried to shape something. It was a joy! Of course, it takes a lot of study, training and mastery of the mind to do this. Helped by the three instructors, we managed to mold three roses,

Live in the Spirit World

which soon disappeared. Two were pink and the third, half red, half yellow.

We laughed a lot.

Blue Flower, invited to take part in the class and give us a demonstration, smiled and did not mince his words. Calmly, he sat down crossing his legs like the logs, mentalized for a few minutes, and a brown box showed up. A kind of jewelry box. What's inside? Marcela asked.

- Can we open it? - asked Nair, curious.

With Blue Flower's permission, we opened it. Inside, there was a plaque, like wood, with the following words engraved on it: "Wisdom is the source of prudence." We clapped our hands, he was embarrassed.

- Beautiful! - we said enthusiastically.

We learned how much can be done with the mind and that we are all capable. It is enough to study and want!

- When giving a pass, does the passer influence who receives it? - James asked Raimundo.

- In a way, yes, it influences me forever. Passes are transfusions of energy. They are donations and, for that to happen, the one who gives the passes must have something to donate. Whether in the Spiritist Centers or with good people who bless, or those who give passes, there are always good disincarnated people next to them who help with these donations.

Live in the Spirit World

- Are the passes useful? - asked Gloria

- Yes, very much so. For sick people they are very useful. For obsessed people, they are of great help. For mediums who do not work with their mediumship, it's like taking a pill for a headache, the effect is cut off for a certain time, but the cause is not eliminated. The pass should be a powerful remedy and, like all remedies, should not be abused. It's not right to become accustomed to passes and become pass-passes and take them for the sake of taking.

- I have heard that if they do not do good, they do no harm - said Rosalia.

- You are wrong. It's just good. We should not underestimate something so useful and serious that demands so much from the passer. Passes are wonderful. So much so that conscious spiritists take courses, study and practice such an event. And it should be more highly valued.

We learned to give passes before visiting the hospital in the Colony, and that was in the first class. It's simple, but we must be aware that we are passing on what we have. We, discarnate, can give passes to incarnates, although they aren't going to be like the ones you could receive from a medium, because we don't have material fluids, but they are always of great help.

We learn to fluidize water. In the Spiritist Centers, and in general for the people who frequent them, it's only a source of energy. The incarnate should always leave clean water for this. Whenever impurities are found, they should

Live in the Spirit World

be neutralized. There is separate water for certain people where they put the medicines they need. The medical team always does this, but as there are many who usually need help, then we learn to be helpful there.

These classes, although short, were of immense benefit.

17.- EARTH'S CREATION

We have seen in movies, in theory class, the creation of the Earth in its different historical epochs, all so beautiful! Tapes that were psychometrically recorded from Earth. I had seen them in video rooms before, but it was different with friends and instructors explaining. All of God's creation is fantastic. The Earth has gone through many transformations, but it's still beautiful.

The unknown fascinates us, both the past and the future. We rarely value the present, which is really the only reality we can all live with. At the level of knowledge, it's necessary to go back to the past for us to have a sense of cosmic evolution. During this course, with gratitude of satisfaction, we were shown and explained a little about our spaceship, planet Earth. We listened very attentively to the explanation about the beginnings of the Earth and humans, rooted in it. We saw its first inhabitants and how religions came about. There is a need for faith in all of us. The spirit knows of the existence of the Creator. We spent several hours looking at the Earth, our blessed home, without getting tired, enraptured by so much beauty. This lesson was so interesting that we did not want to leave the classroom if there was something to know.

Live in the Spirit World

We saw the religions of the past. The idolatry of nature's gods, such as the Sun and the Moon. The emergence of gods made of clay and metal, the wars, the atrocities in the name of religions, which called themselves the owners of the truth, and many cruelties occurred in the context of religion. Then, we studied the current religions in general, just to get an idea of how they believe, act and what their objectives are.

However, we must be careful with some religions that lead to fanaticism. Religions are arrows on the road, but it is up to us to walk.

There are many Christian religions, based on the teachings of Jesus, which are interpreted in various ways. But few of them try to follow the essence of his teachings, restricting themselves to external acts. The ones that facilitate the evolutionary path are those that teach by reasoning, making people understand and believe. Among these is Spiritism, which teaches why God is just, through the laws of reincarnation and the law of cause and effect. It also explains what happens when you are disincarnated.

The class was so well explained that there was no need to ask questions.

We were going to start the practical part and we were doubly happy, because we were going to spend twenty-four hours touring two other countries: India and the Vatican.

We came to Earth by airbus. We visited various temples of our religion and saw their services. A sincere prayer is heard in any service. There are good people of faith in all religions... We love to see, to hear prayers.

Live in the Spirit World

People who pray sincerely are surrounded by pleasant fluids. We listen to their teachings and feel good in their temples. How good religious teachings are! In many temples we were received by the disincarnated. Many, when they are disincarnated, remain in the temples to work, others unfortunately do not know their condition, but do not harm others. Those were the ones we tried to help. But we were are not there for that, but to understand the various faiths.

If there are good people within religions, there are also bad people. There are those who use belief to be dishonest.

Many bad people make mistakes in the name of God, of Jesus. But it's good that the good facts outweigh the bad. All religions teach how to love God, do good and avoid evil.

We've gone to several cults of different religions and they always welcomed us well. We respected everyone, we were quietly paying attention.

We visited the Umbandistas. Sometimes Umbanda is misunderstood. Most of them do good, but unfortunately there are those who call themselves umbandista and don't follow the level of the majority. Their rituals are beautiful, with very meaningful songs. Raimundo greeted them warmly. He's well known, he's always bringing students to meet them. He asked permission and we were kindly led to a hall for visitors dressed in white. We stood and watched. They are very helpful. All but a few of the discarnate working there. They are very patient with the incarnates and do their best to help. We respect Umbanda and its work.

We went to see the Candomblé. The disincarnated followers treated us very well, they even gave a gift to

Live in the Spirit World

Raimundo, who thanked us with a smile. It's a copy of his book. Their rituals are different. We saw everything in silence. They don't like intrusions and it wasn't up to us, the visitors, to make guesses. Their clothing has meaning, their necklaces, in short, everything they wear. Their discarnate have their own Colonies, cities on the Doorway, where there are hospitals, schools, good libraries, and they help each other. There are several Colonies throughout Brazil.

That is where Quimbanda is. She does not give permission to see their rituals. They are groups of incarnates who unite with disincarnated who, for some time, follow other paths.

These groups of incarnates act in this way almost always to make life easier for them. But this help is illusory. They exchange favors each other and make many mistakes.

We saw, from afar, incarnates and reincarnates doing sorcery and bewitchment work. We noticed dark entities, who live in the cities of Doorway, who come to receive the offerings.

These separations are rare after reincarnating. Here, we saw Candomblé helping only his followers and some of his admirers. The followers of Candomblé don't accept the guidelines of the existing Colonies, which is why they created their own nuclei. In the future there will be unity, with the spiritual growth of all.

We know that evil exists, it has strength, but good has much more.

We also saw thank offerings of thanks, and we were able to approach these meetings. They are almost like

Live in the Spirit World

promises, they ask, they receive and donate. Others are just satisfied with how they receive it.

We went on a long-awaited visit abroad. First, India, land of mysticism.

- This is the first time I am going abroad! - Gloria exclaimed happily.

- Me too - I answered.

We did not go to see the spiritual plane, but the material plane. Its temples are enchanting. We learned that Gandhi is in the spiritual space of India, working for his beloved country. In a short time, I could see a few things. Indians are almost always very religious, their religions, unlike Christian religions, are the subject of much controversy. Sacred places have a very strong energy and are protected by countless disincarnated people.

Visiting some like this one, and in a beautiful temple, it was written in Indian, on the spiritual plane, which was translated for us, "God, who is everywhere, is present here through the demonstration of love."

We found everything beautiful. We flew from India to the Vatican. When we got there, a disincarnated team analyzed our visitor's permit and only then allowed us to enter - explained Mrs. Isaura -, because the Vatican is the target of innumerable attacks.

Uncountable suffering and wandering spirits go there in search of help, and most are rescued at the entrance gates. The Vatican is surrounded on the spiritual plane. There are several guards and rescuers working there helping.

Live in the Spirit World

We visited the places allowed to incarnate visitors. The material beauties are numerous. Catholicism inherited much from the pagan religions. Some images of saints were once pagan idols. In places of faith and prayer, the fluids are pleasant. We learned that changes will soon take place in Catholicism.

We saw many rescuers at work, attending to or receiving requests from the incarnate, in unceasing work. Several of them. They were of religious incarnates.

Too bad that these excursions were short, they only gave us the opportunity to visit the material part. But they were unforgettable, I found everything beautiful!

We returned to Brazil, our region, and went to see some Spiritist Centers. The simplicity, and the understanding of the truth, make these humble places become sources of blessing and light. As I was a Spiritist when I was incarnated, it was with great joy that I visited the Spiritist Centers. I love Spiritism!

In the Centers we visited, we were well received. Everyone knew Raimundo and Mrs. Isaura, who were hugged with affection. There, we could ask questions at will. My companions asked numerous questions. I only looked at everything with love. Those were super pleasant excursions.

18.- CONFERENCE AND THE SPIRITIST BOOK FAIR

I rejoiced immensely when we went to the Spiritist Center where my father works. Seeing friends was good for my heart. The meeting started, and there were many incarnate and discarnate people listening to the evening's lecture to hear my father. As he always does, he speaks with clarity and a pleasant voice:

- If we want to get closer to God, we must investigate to know a little about His way of being.

"Human activities have, in the desire for acquisition, the element that sustains them. As a result, we are all selfish, reaching mental or psychic levels."

"Our unconscious or semiconscious brothers, seeking the preservation of the individual, don't go beyond what is necessary for their survival and the fulfillment of their functions. In these manifestations, we can see the Creator God acting without interference in the individual's freedom, something that does not happen in the realm of the human being. Now, if I want to get on well with an individual, I must know him, and like the same things he likes, love what is his, and, if possible, think like him."

Live in the Spirit World

"Why are flowers beautiful and fragrant? It's an interesting question that leads us to meditate and, meditating, we arrive at intuition. For personality, everything has a reason; every path or every action has an end. We cannot conceive of acting without a personal end. We are living in the activity of the mind, an archive of the collective and private past. That is why we do not realize that cosmic action has no need to reach any place, gain or end."

"Many will say that flowers are beautiful and fragrant because God wanted to beautify and perfume the environment and people's lives. What a claim! The beauty, purity and fragrance of the innocent flower also adorn the existence of the angry, the joker, the selfish, the inhuman who can oppose the Creator, who sustains him in all his needs. Moreover, for the Father, who truly loves, the external aspects don't change his way of loving. He loves all their manifestations, because they're part of Him. In fact, it's Himself, because nothing exists outside of Him. No, it wasn't because of man that God created the flowers."

"Why is there so much perfume and beauty for them? Nothing. Whatever they are, they are what they are, by their own inner nature, whether they see it or not. These may be in a garden among men or in the forest where no one sees them. No matter where they are born, they will always be a manifestation of pleasing beauty."

"In the same way, they must be men, only with one difference, what the flower is by innocence, must be man by wisdom. A man has the freedom to be the most beautiful manifestation of the Eternal. Some are against it, and that is what happens with the majority. Others, free and conscious

Live in the Spirit World

of the Divine, integrate with Him, beginning to reflect the Eternal, saturating the Earth with light, beauty, perfume and, above all, with the unconditional love that everything implies in its protective affection."

"What about the violets? Are they envious of roses or would they like to become roses one day? No! The violets are happy to be what they are; happy to be manifestations of the Creator, without claiming any justice from Him who is all, for all that they belong to Him and they possess nothing of themselves."

"'The good man must be good, for that's his nature, and not receive rewards and praise. It doesn't matter whether others see his goodness or not. He must be like the flowers, which don't choose a place or ask for recognition for what they really are."

"We must imitate flowers, whose joy and happiness lies in the permanent attitude of reflecting the beautiful, the fragrant, the imponderable. Paradise is neither here nor here nor there, it is within us."

- What a beautiful lecture! - Ivo exclaimed.

- You should be proud of your father, eh, Patricia? - James said, smiling.

Only I smiled. Yes, I was happy and embarrassed by the compliments of my classmates on my father's beautiful talk.

Finally, a fine shower of salutary fluids filled the room, saturating us with energy. I cried with emotion, I love my parents and to see them studying, working for good makes

Live in the Spirit World

me very happy. To know that they are in communion with the Father is happiness for me. The meeting ended very profitably. We stayed there for a few moments talking.

Mauricio hugged me affectionately:

- And so, how are you, my girl?

- Delighted with the course - I answered.

We returned to Colony where we spent a few free hours. I took the opportunity to write down what I had heard, what I had learned in the course and read a little.

The next morning, we went to visit several bookstalls and Spiritist bookstores. How beautiful!

Standing among good books is always pleasant.

- Spiritist book stalls and bookshops are guarded twenty-four hours a day - Raimundo explained -. When the spiritist book began to stand out, to educate and teach, the darkness began to attack. So, we had to defend ourselves. The worker or workers not only exercise the function of a watchman, but guide, by intuition, sellers and buyers, to clean the environment.

- If you receive an attack from a phalanx, from a large group, what does the worker do? - Lauro asked.

- Almost always - answered Raimundo -, these attacks are predicted, and the teams that work in Spiritist Centers come here. If it was not possible to find out before, when he is surrounded, the worker activates an alarm and in seconds receives help.

- They are the angels of the books - said Zé -, in a good mood. After being there, we went to visit a Spiritist Book Fair.

Live in the Spirit World

If the incarnated work to organize them, the work of the disincarnated isn't a small thing. A discarnate counselor came to receive us kindly.

- You just make yourself comfortable

- How is your work? - Luis asked.

The advisor was kindly enlightened. He is a spirit of unlimited sympathy. Known among the incarnated and disincarnated, he is very fond of good literature. Unfortunately, it is not possible for us to tell his name because, as he said, his work is temporary. He will soon leave it to do another...

We are happy with what we do, we're a group of fifty spirits. We coordinate fairs all over Brazil. When the organization of a fair begins, we have a smaller group that goes to the incarnations, to help them form the bases and protect them. When they start setting up their stalls, we are helping. As the incarnates rotate, so do we.

- What is your role at the fair? - Gloria asked.

- First, to watch, to protect from the attacks of the brethren who are upset by the light that Christian teaching always brings. We are here to guide, give passes, purify the environment, to help the disincarnated who come to accompany the incarnated, and those who come looking for help.

- If two or more fairs occur at the same time, what do you do? - Luíza asked

- The team of fifty is huge, and that's how we are so that we can share ourselves out. But if necessary, the Colony

Live in the Spirit World

The Writer's House, whose inhabitants work for good literature, sends us more helpers. The fairs are growing, and we hope that in the future all cities will have them.

- And when there is no fair? - asked Zé.

- We are not doing nothing, we are always helping people who somehow deal with spiritist newspapers and their publishers, and we encourage people to read, etc.

- What a beautiful job! - I exclaimed.

- Are all the workers here on the team? - Rosalia asked.

- No, we have a team from the city who help us, who come to join us in a collective and pleasant task. In every city where the Spiritist Book Fair takes place, the local workers organize themselves to work extra to help the incarnate ones.

- Are you on duty too? - Ilda asked

- Yes, so that everyone participates and because many of us have other jobs with Spiritist literature.

We look at the books, delighted.

- The incarnated who wish, can have these beautiful works that guide, comfort and explain - said Mrs. Isaura.

We watched for hours. Now the workers sensed the sellers, now they helped the buyers and the visitors. Many disincarnated people were there, sometimes accompanying the incarnate, sometimes as a curiosity seeker. As the incarnate on duty addresses the visitor, the worker politely addresses the discarnate and a dialog ensues; almost always the discarnate is taken to help or to one of the city's Spiritist Centers for guidance.

Live in the Spirit World

Seen from afar, the Fair is a bright spot, where the suffering come for help.

- We have already had a strange form of attack - a worker told us -. The residents of the Doorway gathered a large group of wandering, suffering spirits and brought them to us, hoping that they would spoil the place. But when they saw the light emitted by the Fair, they knelt to ask for help. A counselor went to them, explaining their situation as disincarnated and their need for help, and prayed with them. Everyone was rescued without any problems. Thereafter, they haven't made this type of attack.

We saw a small group of Doorway brothers watching the Fair from a distance.

- What will they do if they approach? - Cida asked the advisor.

- Let's talk to them, we always welcome any visitor. If they attack us, the ray launchers will work; if the attack is bigger, immediately the good workers of the city come to our aid, besides the tent is surrounded by thousands of helpers.

- That's very interesting - said Marcela. - Marcela said. Are there many attacks?

- At the first fairs there were more. Now there are hardly any. They prefer to discourage the incarnate organizers, but the spiritist is stubborn and, when it comes to doing good, to holding the Fair, many firmly resist with our encouragement.

Live in the Spirit World

If the incarnated people like the fair, the disincarnated people who work there like it even more. There reigns joy and affection.

How many aids and help are provided at a fair! And the most important thing: how many good books circulate and teach! We came back excited; the conclusion of the class was just dialogues. Everybody loves to visit the Spiritist Centers, bookstores, kiosks and, mainly, the Spiritist Book Fair.

19 - ADDICTIONS

Mrs. Isaura began the class by talking about addictions in general, and gave a definition:

- Addiction is the habitual use of anything and everything that causes us harm. It is the habit of proceeding badly. Addiction is a complex disease that requires the will to get rid of it. To heal, it is necessary to face it and overcome it; if it is not defeated, it becomes your slave. We will only be free if we do not have addictions. They are all harmful to those who have them. Sometimes one or two we have had obscured the virtues we have acquired.

Our instructor paused and continued:

- There are many vices, and sometimes we do not have them strong, but even a little of them bothers us very much. I will cite the best known: aggression, alcohol, ambition, material attachment, avarice, slander, jealousy, anger, smoking, gluttony, nonconformity, envy, gambling, malice, lies, idleness, pride, pornography, complaining, stealing, addiction, usury, vanity. I don't think we need to describe them. But, if anyone wants to ask a question about one, feel free.

- I did not think that aggression was an addiction - said Ivo.

Live in the Spirit World

- There are people who, when nervous, lash out and cause harm to those around them. They have a bad habit of being violent. The worst thing is that many aggressors do not recognize that they are addicts.

- I knew a lady - said Rosalia -, who used to complain all the time when she was incarnate. She became unpleasant. Whatever subject was spoken to her, she would find a way to introduce disease into the conversation, and the complaining would begin.

- We must be careful not to complain, not only because we are unpleasant to those who listen to us, but because our sorrows only tend to increase and, seeing only the bad things, we forget about the good.

- My father was an alcoholic - Luis said. He was disincarnated because of the problems that drinking caused him. He suffered a lot when he was disincarnated. For years he wandered around the Doorway, crazy about drinking and wanting to take possession of incarnates so he could get drunk with them. It was so sad! He deformed his perispirit, he looked like an animal, until my grandmother, his mother, was able to help him. He is in a hospital in another Colony. He hurt his perispiritual brain so much that I do not think he will reincarnate perfectly.

- It is true, Luis - said Mrs. Isaura. When we damage what we have that is perfect through addictions, we can reincarnate with deficiencies to learn. But this fact is not a general rule. Your father, rescued, can recover.

- But when you are incarnated you can become an alcoholic again, right? - Luis asked again.

Live in the Spirit World

- We only get rid of addiction when we prove ourselves capable. If by choice, we are willing to fight and beat it. In the next incarnation, you may have the will, even though you have suffered, and the pain, this wise companion, has made you averse to drinking. I know a spirit who in the past incarnation was an alcoholic; she disincarnated, suffered and today is an excellent medium, she does not even like the smell of alcoholic beverages.

- Did she overcome her addiction? - I asked

- Yes, she overcame it. The pain made her learn.

- Do all addictions lead to pain? - Lauro asked.

- It also depends on the damage they can cause. Example: if we smoke in an open place and away from other people, we only hurt ourselves. If it's slander, you can harm others. There are vices that are not accentuated and have not caused any major damage, others are strong, ingrained and cause a lot of damage.

- I have a sister who was born mute. I felt so sorry for her. - Nair said sadly. When I disincarnated, I wanted to know why. This fact bothered me a lot because I thought it was unfair.

My father, who had been disincarnated for a long time, said that she had been a slanderer in her previous incarnation. He caused a lot of intrigues, harming many. She disincarnated, suffered much and destructive remorse damaged her vocal cords, and she reincarnated mute.

- As has already been said, he who abuses the perfect may have a deficiency for a time. Each case is different. Not

Live in the Spirit World

all mute people were slanderers. The causes may be different for the same effect.

- Will she talk when she is disincarnated? - Nair asked.

- It will depend on it; if she is good in this reincarnation, she will have help and will soon be talking. If she is not, she will wander or go to the Doorway, remaining silent until she is rescued.

- I have a friend - said Joaquim - who is currently working with me at the Aid Station. He told me that he suffered a lot when two addictions disincarnated him, gambling and smoking.

He was disincarnated and wanted to continue smoking and playing cards. He fears that, when he reincarnates, he will continue the addictions.

- You should not reincarnate with fear. Tell him, at the next opportunity, to continue working, and, if possible, to study. Only reincarnate when you are sure

- When he is sure he will not fall into addiction again? - Joaquim asked.

- It is an extra guarantee. If even the most prepared can make mistakes again, imagine those who think they will succumb.

During the practical class, we went to visit, in the Colony, the wing of the hospital where those detoxing from tobacco and alcohol are. They are all separated. First, we went to visit those undergoing treatment to detox from smoking and who were good people, some spiritists. The visit was pleasant, they were all aware of both their reincarnating and

Live in the Spirit World

their treatment. We saw that everyone was a bit ashamed for not getting rid of the addiction when they were incarnated.

- They stay here for a while - said Frederico.

The second ward was for alcoholics. Unfortunately, alcohol damages the perispirit much more. We talked to some of them and encouraged them. One lady told me:

- I am ashamed to have gone so far downhill from an addiction. Incarnate, I abandoned my parents, husband and children. I did not care about affections, or anyone. I was discarnate and suffered. Until, tired, I remembered God, and for a long time I cried out for help. But, you know, I am still not well, I want to drink.

She cried, and I felt sorry for her. We gave her a pass. When I concentrated on her, I saw that she was distressed, wanting to get drunk.

- It's like that at first - Raimundo explained -. But you'll soon feel better. The Colony will provide her with healthy goals and there is nothing like a good and serious goal to help you forget and overcome an addiction.

The infirmary where the newly-arrived who were addicted to alcohol are kept is a cause for sadness. All of them were marked in such a way that their perispirits were deformed. We prayed and gave them passes, but most of them were oblivious, with stunned looks on their faces.

- Do not reincarnate with fear. Tell him, at the next opportunity, to continue working, and, if possible, to study. He will only be able to reincarnate when he is sure.

Live in the Spirit World

- When he is sure he will not fall into addiction again? - Joaquim asked.

- It is an extra guarantee. If even the most prepared can make mistakes again, imagine those who think they will collapse.

In the practical class, we went to visit, in the Colony, the hospital ward where those detoxing from tobacco and alcohol are kept. All are separated. First, we went to visit those who have a treatment to get detoxified from smoking and who were good people, some spiritists. The tour was enjoyable, everyone was aware of both their disincarnating and their treatment. We saw that they were all a bit ashamed for not getting rid of the addiction when being incarnated.

- They are staying here for a while - said Frederico.

The second ward was for alcoholics. Unfortunately, alcohol damages the perispirit much more.

We talked to some of them and encouraged them. A madam said to me:

- I am ashamed to have so succumbed to an addiction. Incarnate, I abandoned my parents, husband and children. I did not care about affections, or anyone. I was discarnate and suffered. Until, tired, I remembered God, and for a long time I cried out for help. But, you know, I am still not well, I want to drink.

She cried, I sympathized. We gave her a pass. When I focused on her, I saw that she was distressed, wanting to get drunk.

Live in the Spirit World

- " It is like that at first - Raimundo explained -. But soon she will feel better. The Colony will provide her with healthy goals and there is nothing like a good and serious goal to help her forget and overcome an addiction.

The infirmary where the new arrivals who were addicted to alcohol are kept is a reason for sadness. All were marked in such a way that the perispirits were deformed. We prayed and gave them passes, the majority were oblivious, with stunned looks on their faces.

The drug addicts are in a separate hall of the hospital. It is locked, and they cannot leave without permission.

In the backyard that is part of this wing are those who are about to be discharged. We joined them. Their peri spirit was already reconstituted and so we talked. Wanting to know what the other facilities were like in the Colony where we studied. Neither like to talk about themselves or about drugs. This fact brings back bad memories. Then we went to see those in the rooms. It is not nice to look at them. Many young people were there, deformed, some with animal aspects, mostly demented, others did not even speak, they howled. It is difficult to dialogue with those in this state, who don't understand.

- Frederico - asked Gloria -, Are they all recovering?

- Unfortunately, they do not. Many of these brothers not only suffered from drug addiction, but were also aggressive, slanderous, lazy, and made many mistakes; the destructive addiction and remorse have damaged the perispirit so much that we cannot recover from them being

Live in the Spirit World

disincarnated. Only a new body, in material matters, will help them.

- Will they do it as disabled people? - Gloria asked, astonished.

- Yes, they will be handicapped themselves. Reincarnation will be a blessing that will cure them.

We visited a part of the school where there is psychological counseling that helps to release addictions, but for drug addicts there is a special hall in the hospital. It was very interesting; the counselors are very kind and knowledgeable. They are by appointment only. Since we did not want to interrupt or disturb the counselors, the visit was quick. Raimundo commented:

- Everyone always has help, which makes it easier for us to quit the vice. It's just a matter of wanting to.

A gentleman in the waiting room knew Raimundo and went to greet him. Very kindly, he greeted us smiling and said:

- God help that none of you go through what I went through. I have suffered a lot from lying. I am horrified to lie and feel suffocated just thinking about doing it again. I'm in treatment here at school. I want so much to free myself from the vice of lying, and from the horror I have of doing it again. I must balance myself.

When we left, Marcela commented to Raimundo:

- Can the horror of lying again cause you harm?

- Yes, you can, to hate, to feel horror, is not good, not at all. We must avoid vices with understanding. It's not easy

Live in the Spirit World

to give up an addiction, you first must realize that you have it and then do everything possible to get rid of it.

When we are incarnate, we show that we are freed from it, or we strive to fight it. This man fears that when he reincarnates, he will lie again and suffer all over again. But, with the guidance he is receiving, he will have a great opportunity to understand and learn. Whoever learns and puts it into practice overcomes addiction.

We didn't come to see addicts incarnate. It would be easier to see those without addiction, since there are very few.

Vices are still, unfortunately, part of people's lives.

We returned to the classroom to watch films on toxic substances. We learned about the plants that contain them, how they are refined. We saw how drugs travel through the body and what happens to the brain; how one becomes dependent.

- How drugs are so bad for the body and the spirit! - Cida exclaimed, sadly -. How drugs make slaves!

Then we saw many nuclei, cities on the Doorway, where drug addicts gather. These centers are usually not very decorated, but very closed, it's not easy to get in or out of there. The films were made by rescuers who went undercover and filmed everything. They are surrounded by high and strong walls; their buildings have few windows and almost all of them have bars; what is terrible are the warehouses where the prisons are located.

In these centers, there are bosses who are almost always not drug addicts; there are many guards and scholars

Live in the Spirit World

on the subject. There are laboratories where research is carried out. There are ballrooms and lecture halls. There is a place they call school, where they learn to take advantage, to obsess, to take revenge, to intuit the intolerant incarnates to use drugs. The centers always have libraries, where, in addition to the terrible literature, you can find many books and magazines about drugs. These centers are destined to encourage and exercise addictions such as smoking, alcoholism and sexual abuse. Everything is dirty and repulsive.

In Brazil, there are groups like this, of different sizes. The largest are those in the spiritual space of the city of Rio de Janeiro and São Paulo.

I understood why drugs are so deforming. A drug addict doesn't care about anything, he gets more and more decomposed.

We saw many nuclei and I was very sorry.

- Here are Marcelo and Fabio, two former drug addicts, former residents of Valley of the Dolls. They have come to answer some questions and talk to us.

It was a pleasant surprise, they were both young, cheerful and friendly. Fábio said right away:

- I was like that before I got addicted, then I became a human rag. I became a drug addict. I have lived in Valle for a long time. But my family, very Catholic, prayed with faith for me. Prayer came to me to enlighten me, giving me flashes of clarity, then I wanted to change. Then one day, when we were taking advantage of a young man, the group and I were surrounded by a group of students like yourselves. I asked

Live in the Spirit World

for help, they took me to the hospital, admitted me and treated me for a long time. Now I am serving the community that hosted me.

- What did you feel when you were in the valle? - Gloria asked.

- All I could think about was getting high. Disincarnated, I felt the lack of the drug more. I did everything they said to get the drug.

- Were you very deformed? - Ivo wanted to know.

- Yes. One day, when I was in a room with an incarnated man, so we could enjoy cocaine together, I looked in the mirror and was startled. I had little memory of my healthy state.

- Marcelo, and what happened to you, how did you fall into addiction? - Rosalia asked.

- I was a bit lost, idle and I joined other addicts. I was high on my own for two and a half years.

I died of an overdose. They took me to the Valley. I thought it was terrible and, at first, I did drugs, but not much, just to deal with the anguish of being there. Then, I didn't want any more and tried to escape, I was caught and tortured. It was horrible, I suffered a lot. One day, some undercover rescuers came in, they did that periodically and they would release me.

As I wanted to get rid of the addiction, the treatment was fast and soon I was cured.

- What else did you feel after all this? - Marcela asked.

- The pain I caused my parents.

Live in the Spirit World

Addiction is a terrible habit, and the consequences are very sad. For hours the two of them were talking to us.

Afterwards, we visited the local Aid Station, where they are rescued, and there, the drug addicts stay there for the first few days. It's called a Support Station. Many workers are living there. It's not big, but it has fences and big lightning rods. This Station is very much under attack. It is located at the Doorway. We went by airbus. Its backyard is beautiful, flowery, it has blue flowers that resemble hydrangeas and are delicate. It has many benches, where the workers rest. It has a reading room, cafeteria, living quarters for workers and rooms, spacious and very clean. The refugees are separated according to their status. There aren't many houses there, since after a while they are moved to the Colony. When there are vacancies, they receive help from other places. Recently rescued addicts are separated according to their situation. The beds for the restless, agitated ones are covered with magnetic sheets that hold the patient to the bed, without depriving him of movement. We helped the workers to clean and feed them. Many didn't even speak, howling like animals.

To help the intoxicated, you always need a lot of workers. Which is why at the Colony they are always encouraging everyone's cooperation. That's why during the leaves and vacations of the workers of the Colonies and Stations, such as teachers, doctors, etc., and many others join these servants unselfishly, they're like crowds that help the imprudent brothers who have fallen into addiction.

The help is not easy, because the addict almost always does not want to give up the addiction.

Live in the Spirit World

We ourselves went with a great desire to help, we worked hard and got few results, but that made us happy.

In the concluding class we did not have much to ask. It was an easy subject to understand, but very difficult to achieve. There are few liberated, many trying to free themselves and a large part, slaves of addictions.

20.- ACKNOWLEDGMENTS

The day dawned beautifully, like every day at the Colony. Our last class was about to take place: our course was over. I was thoughtful. On my mental screen, the events we had lived through appeared, like in a movie. A tender emotion welled up in my soul. I loved everyone, and at that moment I felt that it was not the same affection for everyone. I thought of one at a time and saw with great joy that God, in creating us, did not make copies, but gave us the ability to love indistinctly, seeing the special values that stand out in each one. In one, he especially loved their spontaneity; in another, ability for selflessness; in another, simplicity; in another, kindness; and in many, intelligence. In this way, the natural qualities of each person shone in my eyes. And it seemed to me that love, seeing it in this way, multiplied within me, even though there wasn't a way to measure it.

When I remembered the teachers, I felt a deep respect. How could I show my gratitude for everything they had done for me, for all the knowledge they had and passed on to us?

Acknowledgement? No! It was too little for how much they had done for us. There was not payment for this kind of acquired property, the least I could do was to have them as an example. From now on, all my thoughts and attitudes

Live in the Spirit World

would be based on the virtues they demonstrated during the time we were together.

My heart overflowed with love and affection, I was happy. It's not the happiness that, in the material, we look for as synonymous with power, comfort and idleness. The happiness I felt was the result of a burning desire to work, to serve, to love intensely all the manifestations of my God, because He is everything to me, and I saw it in all my friends, brothers and teachers.

The goodbyes began, and I felt it deeply. Some of our group would change jobs, enthusiastic about other ways to serve. All the requests for change were accepted, making us happy. Only Lauro, Laís and I would continue studying. But we would also be separated. They would both go to one study colony, and I would go to another.

- What are you going to do, Patricia? - Nair asked.

- I will spend the days I have free with Grandma and visiting my relative Then I will go back to study.

I am looking forward to learning and getting to know people.

I memorized the conversation I had with my friend Antônio Carlos.

- Patricia - he said -. I am going to accompany you to a Study Colony, where you'll take a deeper course on the spiritual plane and the Gospel.

He spoke enthusiastically about this Colony.

- It's beautiful, you will find great friends there. It's one more step; afterwards, I want to take you to the Writer's

Live in the Spirit World

House. It's a place where you will study, learn to read and write, to dictate to the incarnated brothers everything you see and learn.

- You really like the Writer's House, don't you? - I asked

- Yes, I love this place. It's a Colony where brothers who love to learn and teach come together in a mutual effort to spread good literature. It's wonderful!

In the classroom, we talked for half an hour, happy and sad at the same time. Everyone felt the completion of their studies. But we were happy to have completed it. No one could say that one was still the same as before, we felt enriched.

Mrs. Isaura and Raimundo would soon welcome another class. Frederico would return to his Colony of Study, where he would teach a determined subject in the Medicine course.

- And Blue Flower?

Upon being reminded, this friend entered the room.

- I beg your permission to be with you in these last moments.

I hugged him for a long time. I has rehearsed a formal thank you beforehand, but I felt so emotional that I only managed to say:

- Thank you!

He smiled gently and wiped the two stubborn tears that came out of my eyes on my face.

Live in the Spirit World

- Now, Patricia's Blue Flower, I am back to my regular job, full time. With lots of earnings.

I made more friends. We hugged and promised to see each other.

Raimundo asked for silence. Our instructor friend did not have much to talk about. With a smile on his lips, he looked at us warmly:

- Friends, I thank you for making this course a great learning experience, for making this work a help to other brothers. Acquired knowledge is our goods, treasures that enrich us. It was a pleasure to spend time with you. I hope you will put into practice what you have learned in these months of living together. We can help, it's wonderful. Now, let's unite our thoughts in acknowledgment to the Father, to whom we owe everything.

Acknowledgement must be within each one of us.

He was silent for a moment, letting our thanks be particularized.

"Dad, thank you for everything - I thought -. For everything. I am very happy, I have received so much, help me to always be worthy to continue receiving."

Raimundo, with an emotional voice, prayed to the Lord's Prayer.

Then we cheered with joy I felt happy to have finished another phase, another course of the many that I had longed to take.

End.

Live in the Spirit World
Zibia Gasparetto's Greatest success stories

With more than 20 million titles sold, the author has contributed to the strengthening of spiritualist literature in the publishing market and to the popularization of spirituality. Learn more of the author's successes.

Romances Dictated by the Spirit Lucius

The Life Force

The Truth of each one

Life knows what it does

She trusted in life

Between Love and War

Esmeralda

Thorns of Time

Eternal Bonds

Nothing is by Chance

Nobody is Nobody's

God's Advocate

Tomorrow Belongs to God

Love Won

Unexpected Encounter

On the Edge of Destiny

The Sly One

The Morro of Illusions

Where is Teresa?

Live in the Spirit World

Through the Doors of the Heart

When Life chooses

When the Hour Comes

When it is necessary to return

Opening for Life

Not afraid to live

Only love can do it

We Are All Innocent

Everything has its price

It was all worth it

A real love

Overcoming the past

Other success stories by André Luiz Ruiz and Lucius

The Love Never Forgets You Trilogy

The Strength of Kindness

Under the Hands of Mercy

Saying Goodbye to Earth

At the End of the Last Hour

Sculpting Your Destiny

There are Flowers on the Stones

The Crags are made of Sand

Live in the Spirit World

Live in the Spirit World
Books of Eliana Machado Coelho and Schellida

Hearts without Destiny

The Shine of Truth

The Right to be Happy

The Return

In the Silence of Passions

Strength to Begin Again

The Certainty of Victory

The Conquest of Peace

Lessons Life Offers

Stronger than Ever

No Rules for Loving

A Diary in Time

A Reason to Live

Eliana Machado Coelho and Schellida, Romances that captivate, teach, move and

can change your life!

Live in the Spirit World
Romances of Arandi Gomes Texeira and The Count J.W. Rochester

Lancaster County

The Power of Love

The Trial

Cleopatra's Bracelet

The Reincarnation of a Queen

You Are Gods

Books of Marcelo Cezar and Marco Aurelio

Love is for the Strong

The Last Chance

Nothing is as it Seems

Forever With Me

Only God Knows

You Make Tomorrow

A Breath of Tenderness

Live in the Spirit World
Books of Vera Kryzhanovskaia and JW Rochester

The Revenge of the Jew

The Nun of the Marriages

The Sorcerer's Daughter

The Flower of the Swamp

The Divine Wrath

The Legend of the Castle of Montignoso

The Death of the Planet

The Night of Saint Bartholomew

The Revenge of the Jew

Blessed are the poor in spirit

Cobra Capella

Dolores

Trilogy of the Kingdom of Shadows

From Heaven to Earth

Episodes from the Life of Tiberius

Infernal Spell

Herculanum

On the Frontier

Naema, the Witch

In the Castle of Scotland (Trilogy 2)

Live in the Spirit World

New Era

The Elixir of Long Life

The Pharaoh Mernephtah

The Lawgivers

The Magicians

The Terrible Phantom

Paradise without Adam

Romance of a Queen

Czech Luminaries

Hidden Narratives

The Nun of the Marriages

Books of Elisa Masselli

There is always a reason

Nothing goes unanswered

Life is made of decisions

The Mission of each one

Something more is needed

The Past does not matter

Destiny in his hands

Live in the Spirit World

God was with him

When the past does not pass

Just beginning

Live in the Spirit World
Books of Vera Lúcia Marinzeck de Carvalhoç and Patricia

Violets in the Window
Living in the Spirit World
The Writer's House
Flight of the Seagull

Vera Lúcia Marinzeck de Carvalho and Antônio Carlos

Love your Enemies
Slave Bernardino
the Rock of Lovers
Rosa, the third fatality
Captives and Freed

Live in the Spirit World
Books of Mónica de Castro y Leonel

In spite of everything

Love is not to be trifled with

Face to Face with the Truth

Of My Whole Being

I wish

The Price of Being Different

Twins

Giselle, The Inquisitor's Mistress

Greta

Till Life Do You Part

Impulses of the Heart

Jurema of the Jungle

The Actress

The Force of Destiny

Memories that the Wind Brings

Secrets of the Soul

Feeling in One's Own Skin

World Spiritist Institute

www.ingramcontent.com/pod-product-compliance
Lightning Source LLC
LaVergne TN
LVHW041936070526
838199LV00051BA/2809